"I need  simply

"Not a permanent, legal wife," he continued, "but someone who will act like a wife in every other way. I want that woman to be you."

Charli nearly swallowed her gum. "You want me to pretend to be your wife?"

"Isn't that your business?" Max replied.

"Yes, but…" She paused.

"Professionally, I need a woman at my side."

"And personally?"

"I don't."

Pamela Bauer and Judy Kaye: Four hundred miles separate these two North American authors, but that doesn't stop them from collaborating. Both authors bring a wealth of experience to their collaborative effort. Pamela has written fifteen romances and Judy is the author of forty-five young adult/children's nonfiction and romance titles. Collaborating comes so naturally, they think they might be sisters separated at birth. They have discovered they can read their manuscripts and not know which lines are Judy's and which are Pam's. Each has a tolerant husband, two children and a dog that thinks it's a human.

Look out for *Almost a Father* by these two talented authors, coming in May 1998.

A Wife for Christmas

Pamela Bauer & Judy Kaye

Harlequin Books

TORONTO • NEW YORK • LONDON
AMSTERDAM • PARIS • SYDNEY • HAMBURG
STOCKHOLM • ATHENS • TOKYO • MILAN
MADRID • WARSAW • BUDAPEST • AUCKLAND

ISBN 0-373-03485-7

A WIFE FOR CHRISTMAS

First North American Publication 1997.

PROLOGUE

"I WANT to hire a wife."

Max Talyor's words bounced off Walker Calhoun as hard as his kill shot had zinged off the walls securing his fifteen to zero racquetball victory only minutes ago.

Already winded, Walker spoke in spurts. "There are . . . names . . . for men . . . who do that sort of thing."

"It's not what you're thinking." Max's blue eyes glinted at Walker, who was sprawled in the corner of the racquetball court, his sweat dripping onto the gleaming wood floor. "I answered an ad in the newspaper . . ."

"You're into the personals?" Walker exclaimed in disbelief. "You're in bad shape, my friend, if you're combing the personals for women. Shyness is one thing, but this. . . ." He cautiously moved one foot to see if it was still functioning.

"It wasn't that kind of ad," Max snapped impatiently, dropping nimbly to his friend's side. "It was in the business section. I've hired a service which takes care of all those little things that wives usually do—like plan parties, do your shopping, pick up your laundry. They'll do just about anything.''

Walker raised both of his eyebrows. "Anything?"

Max gave him a disgusted glare. "Wipe that lecherous look off your face. It's a legitimate business called Almost A Wife. The office is on Nicolette Avenue. I haven't got the details worked out yet because the idea just occurred to me yesterday."

"And what is it going to cost you to get all these wonderful wifely services?" Walker dabbed at his forehead with his wristband.

"Whatever the cost, it'll be worth the investment." Max tilted his dark head back until it rested against the wall, waiting for Walker to catch his breath before they made their way to the locker room. "I need a wife."

"Do you get to choose which woman you want to be your wife?"

Max scraped his fingers through his crisp dark hair. "Charli McKenna. I'm going with the owner of the service."

"You always do get the best, don't you?"

"I like things done right."

"And she's efficient when it comes to taking care of your shorts and socks?" Walker taunted.

"Laugh all you want. The way I see it, it's a perfect setup. I'll have the convenience of a wife without the emotional ties." He started toward the locker room.

Walker followed shortly, shaking his head. "I never thought I'd see the day when my best buddy *hired* a wife."

Max spun around. "Once you see how efficient my life's going to be, you'll understand."

"Why don't you just get married? There are women standing in line to say 'I do' with you."

Max made a sound of disgust. "Or 'I do' to my wallet. Besides, you know how I feel about marriage. Not now. Not ever. Never."

Walker held up his hands defensively. "I know, I know. I've heard it often enough. But I think a little word of caution might be needed here, old buddy."

"And what might that be?"

"Be careful what you wish for—you might get it."

CHAPTER ONE

CHARLI McKenna whistled through her teeth as she let herself into Max Taylor's Lake of the Isles Tudor home. Her eyes sparkled with satisfaction as she took in the house's elegance. "Tonight is going to be perfect, Max. You just wait and see."

With a bunch of red and white balloons tied to her wrist, she gingerly crossed the slate foyer, peeking into the stately rooms, humming a love song. The house felt far too much like a museum which demanded silence.

"A girl could get lost in a place like this," she murmured. "But it's so beautiful, who would care?"

Everything in the house spoke of class and money. Charli stood back to ponder an original Wyeth on the wall, her thumb on her chin. Wyeth was a favorite of hers, too. She stood for a few minutes longer, contemplating the artwork, then moved away.

"Time to get to work," she told herself as she hitched the balloons to the newel at the foot of the stairs. "You need every minute you've got to make this the most romantic, most intimate, most...memorable night of Max's life."

As she entered the formal dining room, she took one look at the monstrous oak table and knew it wouldn't work. Even with white linen and silver, it would never provide an intimate setting. And that's exactly what tonight had to be—a romantic, candle-lit dinner for two. Max was expecting it and Charli wasn't going to disappoint him.

She found the stereo system and tuned the radio to a country-western station. She pumped up the volume so that she could hear the music as she moved about the mansionlike home. Humming along, Charli dug into the pocket of her jeans and pulled out a small atomizer of perfume and spritzed a little behind each ear. Perfume always put her in the mood for preparing a romantic rendezvous.

In one of the sitting rooms she found a small, round, cherrywood table which would be much more appropriate than the imposing one in the dining room. Charli quickly stuffed the Stiffel brass lamp resting on it into the nearest closet. She carried the table into the living room and positioned it in front of the fireplace.

Library shelves bordering both sides of the mantel boasted an impressive array of reading material. The topics ranged from medicine and pioneering space travel to gourmet cooking and the proper way to grow bonsai trees. Interspersed on the shelves were lovely hand carvings of

African animals—elephants, giraffes, lions and a couple Charli couldn't identify.

"You're no slouch in the intellect or travel departments, are you, Max?" she murmured. "I like that in a man."

Singing along with a country-western tune about the woes of a love gone wrong, she draped an ivory lace cloth over the table. Next came the two place settings of Dresden china, Waterford crystal and sterling silver.

"Co...zy! Max, baby, by the time I've got this place fixed up, there ain't no way any love's gonna go wrong tonight." She affected a Southern drawl as she stood back to admire the effect.

She had brought a beautiful bouquet of tiger lilies and mums for the centerpiece, but now that she was here, she knew the flowers were all wrong. There was only one flower that would suit this occasion—white roses. She glanced at her watch and was mentally calculating whether she had enough time to run to the florist when the doorbell rang.

White-coated caterers stood on the doorstep. Charli led them to the kitchen and outlined their instructions for the evening ahead. She wanted no mistakes—the right menu, the proper serving etiquette and, most importantly, a discreet departure as soon as the meal was over.

While they began their preparations in the kitchen, Charli hurried to the nearest florist in search of two dozen long-stemmed white roses.

"Flowers for the Taylor residence?" the brisk, French-roll-coiffed clerk inquired as she expertly wrapped them in paper and slid them into a box. "We can charge it if you wish. Mr. Taylor has a long-standing account with our store."

"Sends a lot of flowers, does he?" Charli asked in amusement.

"And receives them." The older woman sniffed disdainfully. "Times have certainly changed. In my day, young women would never have thought to send a man flowers but now...." The clerk looked as though these forward women would be the undoing of the civilized world. Charli held back a smile. She didn't have time to pump the woman for information about her new account, so she bundled the flowers into her arms and hurried back to her car.

As she parked her Ford Escort in the back of Max Taylor's house, a sleek, dark Mercedes pulled into the circular drive out front. "Oh, no! It must be him!" Charli exclaimed in a frantic whisper and raced into the house. She ripped the packaging paper from the roses and hurried through the kitchen to the living room. As she set the cut-glass vase on the small round table, she heard the front door open.

Out of breath, Charli slipped into the study and switched the stereo system from the country-western radio station to the CD player. The soft sounds of Vivaldi's Four Seasons filled the house. Charli leaned against the study wall waiting for her heart to stop thumping.

A little rush of disappointment slipped through her as she realized her job was done. Once, just once, she wished she could arrange a romantic rendezvous for herself, not for her clients.

That was the toughest part about owning and running Almost A Wife. She planned the most wonderful parties, the most lavish dinners, the most intimate trysts—and then left before the party began.

"Oh, well," she murmured to herself. "The least I can do is satisfy my curiosity."

Charli tiptoed through the corridor. Flattening herself against the wall, she peeked around the corner to catch a glimpse of the couple in the living room.

But there was no couple. A lone man in the room captured her attention.

Dressed in a dark suit with a crisp white shirt, he emanated power and success. His thick dark hair was frosted with a hint of gray at the temples and trimmed to a short, stylish cut. He had an irresistible smile as he surveyed the room that caused Charli's heart to do a funny little flip-flop.

He seemed pleased by the table in front of the fireplace and the gently licking flames of the fire.

He slipped off his jacket and placed it over the back of a chair. He moved silently through the room, his dark gaze resting on every detail Charli had worked so hard to provide—the crystal, the flowers, the champagne.

When he was through, he walked to a graceful writing desk nearby and punched a button on the answering machine. A woman's voice floated into the room.

"Max, darling, where have you been? I've missed you. Call me? You know the number." The breathless words died away as another message began to play.

"Max, honey, it's Jana. I know you're busy, but I've got tickets to the symphony on Saturday. Interested? We could have dinner and dessert at my place after." There was a pause. "*I* could be dessert if you like...."

Three more messages similar in theme played before he shook his head in disgust and silenced the machine. Charli, just like Alice in Wonderland, grew curiouser and curiouser.

She sighed, filled with an uncharacteristic surge of envy. Whomever was going to share this room...this night...with Max Taylor was one lucky lady.

As she passed a mirror on the wall, she studied herself critically. It was unlikely she'd be the kind of woman Max Taylor might invite to dinner. She looked like an elf with short, unmanageable dark curls. Her skin was a pearly white. Even if she had spent six months in the tropics, she would never have a golden tan. Nor did she need fancy makeup to feel good about herself. She'd always been one of the "guys," comfortable with any group of weekend athletes. Why was it that tonight she wished she looked glamorous?

It must be the house and its owner, Charli concluded, unable to resist admiring the elegant yet practical kitchen. With a sigh, she pulled an invoice from her pocket and set it on the counter. All that was left of her job was a last-minute reminder to the caterers.

She was about to slip out the back door when Max Taylor stopped her. "Ms. McKenna, you're not quite finished yet," he said, his eyes taking in every inch of her appearance and causing Charli to squirm.

"Is something not to your satisfaction?" Her stomach tightened at the thought.

"Everything is perfect."

"Except?" she prodded, knowing there must be something she had overlooked.

"Except that I want you to stay and have dinner with me."

Judging by the way he was looking at her, Charli figured her jaw had probably dropped open before she managed to say, "You want *me* to have dinner with you?"

He smiled then, a most gorgeous smile which made Charli's heart move into a different rhythm altogether. "Is that so unusual a request?"

"Ah . . . yes," she stammered. "You're my client, Mr. Taylor."

"Call me Max." This time the smile was enough to weaken Charli's limbs. Before she could give him an answer, he was helping her out of her jacket. Charli didn't protest.

"I don't understand why you want me to stay . . . Max." When she said his name she thought she saw his eyes darken in satisfaction.

"Let's just say that this evening was a kind of test."

"A test?" she asked weakly as she allowed him to lead her into the living room.

"I've been thinking about using your service on a regular basis. Before I made that decision I wanted to make sure that we would work well together." He pulled out a chair for her and indicated that she should sit.

"If you're satisfied with my work, Mr.—I mean, Max, you don't need to give me dinner in order to hire me to do more." His eyes made her extremely nervous, staring intently into hers as if he had some great secret he wasn't quite willing to share with her.

"Oh, but what a shame it would be to let all this wonderful food and ambience go to waste." He looked about the room appreciatively. "You really are quite good at planning dinner parties."

The compliment warmed Charli, as did the way his voice softened as he spoke. Charli knew it was a voice that had had a lot of experience talking to women, yet she couldn't stop the tingling that spread across her skin at the sound of it.

"Thank you," she murmured, grateful that his attention had turned to the bottle of wine. As he filled her glass with the bubbly liquid, Charli tried to keep her hands from twisting in her lap.

"You aren't married, are you?"

"No."

"Good," he said with a satisfied look.

"Good?"

"I might need your services at odd hours. I wouldn't want to cause problems in a marriage."

"Just what kind of business do you have in mind?"

"Wifely business, of course."

Taylor smiled and Charli was again struck with his incredible handsomeness. "My housekeeper has recently informed me that she needs time off to care for her sister who isn't well. That leaves me in a bind, but I believe Almost A Wife can help me in the interim." He pulled a sheet of paper from his pocket. "Here's a list of the services I require. Do you have any problems with that?"

She scanned the page. There was nothing listed that Almost A Wife hadn't done dozens of times—gift buying, laundry service, party planning, cleaning, grocery shopping—yet something inside her wanted her to drop the paper and run far away from the dangerously attractive man across from her.

"Well, Ms. McKenna?"

"No problem. We can handle it," she told him, wondering just how she would handle a man like Max Taylor.

"Good. I'd like you to begin working for me right away. Christmas is only three weeks away. I need you to take care of my shopping."

Charli hid her disapproval. She never minded buying gifts, but deep in her heart she wished her clients would purchase their own Christmas gifts. It seemed so impersonal to hire a shopper for the holiday she loved best. She forced a weak smile. "Of course. Do you have a list?"

"My secretary can help you with that. She usually bails me out on the twenty-fourth. She'll be as grateful as I am that you're willing to take this on for me." He gave a tiny shudder. "Every year the company grows and the job gets bigger. Still, I appreciate good employees and want them to know that."

Charli admired his attitude and could find no fault with his generosity to herself or to others. She was mulling over the ways in which she could use the money she'd earn from this particular client when he asked, "Any questions?"

"About Christmas...I should start buying gifts immediately. If you'd indicate which ones are family members..."

He shook his head forcefully. "I'll take care of purchasing gifts for my brothers and sister-in-law myself." He smiled apologetically. "Frankly, I enjoy buying gifts for my nephew Jeremy. He's only two."

He went up one notch in Charli's estimation with that statement. Charli busied herself scribbling on the notepad she'd brought with her. She didn't want to think about this new, intriguing client with too much fondness. "Is there anything else?"

"I think that about covers it. Here's to a long, successful relationship, Charli." He lifted his glass to her.

"To business," she said, clicking her crystal glass against his.

He smiled. "I'm going to enjoy your being almost my wife, Charli."

Charli doubted she could say the same.

"Here's a brochure explaining our services, Mr. Hanson. I'm sure that Almost A Wife could be a great help to you." Charli spoke in her most soothing voice to the elderly gentleman across from her. For ten minutes she'd listened to fond recollections of his dearly departed wife and assured him that, though Almost A Wife couldn't replace his spouse, their service could surely make life easier for him.

"We can arrange for laundry pickup, a house-cleaning service, even your dinner meal, if you choose. If you'll give us a list of your children's birth dates and anniversaries we'll make sure that cards, gifts or flowers are delivered on time. We can decorate your home for holidays, organize parties, even make sure the plumber gets in to fix the sink while you're out. We'll see that your car is washed and your magazine subscriptions are renewed. If you need a daily reminder to take your vitamins..."

Mr. Hanson gave a weak smile. "You even 'nag,' if necessary?"

"Ouch." Charli chuckled. "We like to call our telephone service 'helpful reminders.'"

"I like you, Ms. McKenna. And I like the idea of having my life in order again." He sighed. "I hate to admit it, but I took my wife for granted. Now, when I see all the jobs she did printed out on this brochure..."

"You don't have to worry about a thing. We're discreet, nonintrusive and efficient." Charli gave him a broad smile. "And we won't nag unless you ask us to. Now, if you'd like to move to Nita's desk, she'll make note of all the services you wish. If you have any further questions, call anytime."

While Mr. Hanson was finalizing his requirements with her office mate, Charli brewed a fresh pot of almond-flavored coffee and carried it into the office with two cherry tarts. When she entered, Mr. Hanson's eyes misted. "And you're a mind reader, too! Cherry tarts are my favorite. I haven't had them since Bessie died.'' By the time he left, his face was split with a wide smile.

"Well, that was easy," Nita commented. "What a sweet man! He'll be wonderful to work for."

"Makes it all worthwhile, doesn't it?" Charli sighed as she sank into the chair across from Nita's. "I love accepting clients who will truly appreciate our work."

"Makes up for the difficult ones," Nita said bluntly. "Of which there are many." She snapped her fingers. "By the way, Max Taylor called while you were talking to Mr. Hanson. He wanted to remind you of your appointment."

Charli groaned.

"What's wrong? I thought you said he was quite nice the night you had dinner."

"He was, but I'd really rather not get involved with men like Max Taylor."

"Involved? You're working for him, not sleeping with him," Nita reminded her.

"I realize that," Charli snapped. "But I think he wants to put us on retainer."

"That's great! We can use the business."

"I know, but I'd like to think twice on this one."

"Why? I thought you wanted to pay back the loan you took to open Almost A Wife."

Charli scooped her hands through her curly black hair. "I do, but Max is dangerous." Again, she groaned. "Why couldn't he be like the ma-

jority of our clients—nice, safe, married men who
are looking for extra help for their wives?''

''We've had single men before.''

''But those single men didn't have so many
women on their gift lists—they can't *all* be Max's
relatives.''

Nita laughed. ''If I remember correctly, none
of those single men was as good-looking or as
wealthy as Mr. Maxwell Taylor.''

''That's what bothers me.''

Nita's face softened. ''I'm sorry, Charli. I had
forgotten about Griffith.''

''Well, I haven't. I've had my fill of rich,
handsome men who think the world revolves
around them. I vowed I'd never let another seven-
figure man use me again.''

''Griffith Parks was a jerk and treated you
badly, but just because Max Taylor is wealthy
doesn't mean that he's the same kind of man,''
Nita reasoned.

''Nita, maybe *you* should go to Max's office.
Or better yet, we could send Richard.'' Charli
referred to her part-time help, Richard Hughes.

''Sorry, but I've already suggested that to Mr.
Taylor. His words were, 'I prefer to do business
with Ms. McKenna. If she wants the account,
she'll come herself.' Besides that, Charli, you
know we never send Richard on this type of appointment. It wrecks the Almost A *Wife* image
to see a six-foot-two male wander through
the door.''

Charli sighed. "I suppose you're right. Give me that address." She grabbed for the work order. "I'll go right now, before I talk myself out of it."

At that moment, across town, Max was having his own thoughts about Charli as he stared into the huge armoire in his dressing room.

No fresh shirts—again. He looked at his trouser-covered legs and bare chest in the mirror. "That laundry service will have to go," he muttered. "I'll take care of it tomorrow." He paused. "Correction. I'll put it on Charli's list."

She was the only bright spot in an already irritating morning. Now he'd have to stop on the way to work and pick up his clean shirts. His electric razor had broken and he hadn't had time to fix it. As it was, he was shirtless and scarred from a bout with a not-so-sharp, straight-edged razor. He felt as though he'd done battle with a prickly pear and lost. There was that stack of phone messages near the answering machine—all calls to be returned, and all from women.

"If I'd hired Charli earlier, none of this would have happened." He glared into the mirror at the barefoot image glaring back at him. His unzipped trousers drooped low on his hips. He stared ruefully through the mirror at the rumpled bedroom behind him. Charli would save him from all these mundane hassles. His frown dissolved into a grin. This was the best idea he'd had in years!

Charli felt uncharacteristic apprehension building within her as she drove toward downtown Minneapolis. The beautiful and dramatic skyline usually cheered her. But today all she could think of was a handsome dark-haired man with a seductively charming grin who was determined to involve her and Almost A Wife in his life.

Nita didn't think that Max Taylor was like Griffith Parks. Charli wasn't as convinced. She knew there were lots of women in his life. She'd heard the telephone messages on the answering machine. She supposed it was none of her business, but she was still curious—did he know how to be faithful to one woman or was Max Taylor another Griffith?

By the time she'd parked her car in the IDS parking ramp Charli was thoroughly ill-tempered. Thinking about Griffith always did this to her. As she rode the elevator to the thirtieth floor, she practiced her deep breathing relaxation techniques.

The doors whispered open onto a lovely reception area carpeted in persimmon, the walls highlighted with green marble tile. The room felt as though the decorators had packed up and slipped out the back door only moments before. Even the leaves on the plants were still glossy with dew. Almost A Wife couldn't have done better.

"May I help you?" A flawlessly coiffed middle-aged woman spoke from behind a magnificent Art Deco cherrywood desk. Suddenly Charli regretted arriving in her funky floral leggings and baggy purple sweatshirt.

"Max Taylor, please. I'm Charli McKenna. I believe he's expecting me."

"You're Ms. McKenna?" She gave Charli a look of disbelief.

Charli tucked back her shoulders and raised her pert little chin. "Yes, I am. Is something wrong?"

The secretary quickly composed herself. "Not at all. I was expecting someone older, that's all." She smiled warmly and offered Charli her hand. "It's a pleasure to meet you. I'm Dora. Max has told me about you. Quite frankly, I think you're going to be perfect for him."

Charli didn't know what to say other than, "Thank you." Sensing the warmth in the woman's personality, she added, "I suspect you and I will be working together often."

"Together we should be able to manage him, eh?" Dora winked conspiratorially.

Charli nodded politely, wondering if anyone *ever* managed a man like Max. "Shall I go in?"

"Go ahead. He's on the phone with his brother, but should be through any minute."

Charli knocked on the door and stepped inside at his invitation. Max had the telephone receiver tucked beneath his chin, his hands busy sorting

through a stack of files on his desk. She took the
moment to look around. The books looked as
though they were used often. It was a very impressive office; a perfect showcase for Taylor
himself.

He looked good in black. Not many men could
wear an unrelieved black suit without looking like
an undertaker, Charli observed as she waited for
his phone call to end. On Taylor, however, the
black suit and pristine white shirt unleashed an
aura of influence and power.

She settled herself into a chair. From her perch,
Charli couldn't help overhearing Max's end of
the conversation.

"I was thinking about getting Jeremy a train
set."

A brief silence followed.

"What about a remote-controlled car?"

Again silence.

"It probably won't matter to Jeremy. You and
I usually end up playing with the toys anyway."
He glanced toward Charli. "Gotta go. I've got
an appointment. See you on Sunday."

"Sorry about that," Taylor apologized as he
hung up the telephone. "I hope I didn't keep you
waiting long."

"It's all right. I charge by the hour," Charli
quipped, hoping humor would help to diffuse the
odd, pulsing feeling in her stomach.

"Always a businesswoman, even when she's
dressed like a pixie." His eyes studied her

thoroughly and Charli wished she had worn the navy blue suit instead of the purple floral leggings. "Appearance can be deceptive, Mr. Taylor." She felt small and scantily dressed under his gaze.

"Please call me Max."

"Very well, Max." Charli blushed. "About business. How can we help you?"

"After seeing what a thorough and professional job you did for me, I'd like to retain you on a more ... permanent basis."

Charli knew she couldn't turn this opportunity down. "I could put you on our list of regular clients and assign one of my employees to your account."

"I don't want to be on a list, Charli. And I don't want anyone else working with me. I want you."

Unable to stop herself, Charli blushed. "I'm not sure I'm following you, Mr. Taylor." She reverted to his formal name.

"It's very simple, Charli," he answered, emphasizing her name. "I need a wife—not a permanent, legal wife, but someone who will act like a wife in every other way. I want that woman to be you."

Charli nearly swallowed her gum. "You want me to pretend to be your wife?" She was certain that she had misunderstood him.

"Isn't that what your business is all about?"

"Yes, but ..." She paused, at a loss for words.

"Professionally, I need a woman at my side."

"And personally?"

"I don't... Don't look at me that way, Charli. I haven't lost my mind. This is very...complex."

"Obviously." She wasn't going to let him off easily. That, too, was apparent.

"I'm a very busy man. My business has started to grow at a rather alarming rate. I factored in the possibility of significant growth for the company, but this has exceeded any of my advisers' predictions and my own expectations."

"Congratulations are in order, then, I suppose."

Charli's dry comment made him wince. "This is hardly a plea for pity. I just want to make you understand that I have no time for socializing right now—I'm doing everything I can to keep my head above water. Unfortunately, a man in my position is *expected* to make appearances at certain events, to patronize certain charities. I need a wife—especially with the holidays coming...you understand."

"Believe me, I'm trying."

"To be perfectly frank with you, many of my colleagues think that it's time I married, eased back on the work, even started a family."

"How dreadful for you."

"I'm not interested in finding a woman, Charli, and I'm growing very tired of women 'finding' me. It's begun to interfere with the way I live my life."

Charli bit back another sarcastic retort. Amazingly, she believed him. More amazing still, she felt a little *sorry* for him! She'd heard firsthand the way women brazenly chased Max. Those hot and breathy phone messages still resonated in her head. Max was nothing if not polite. Discouraging persistent women could be a problem for someone as careful and as well-bred as Max seemed to be. Still, it was a ridiculous problem—and his solution seemed equally ridiculous.

"Hear me out, Charli. There's more." He could see by the look on her face that he hadn't garnered any sympathy from her. "Men in my position are expected to be 'respectable.' To some, that equates with 'married.' There is a good old boys club at the top and I'm not in it."

"Because you aren't married?"

"Stability. Respectability. Family values. They're still in style. Playboys don't get where I want to be, Charli."

It all made a sort of stupid sense, Charli mused. Max not only had to *be* trustworthy, he had to *appear* trustworthy. And a wife was good for that.

"I see."

"Do you?"

Charli thought she did. He didn't want to commit to one woman. It was obvious from the phone messages she had overheard that there was no shortage of women in his life. Naturally, he wouldn't want a *real* wife, only a pretend one.

"I'll double your salary... in fact, it won't be necessary for you to work for anyone else at all. You can move into the servants' quarters of my house. To the outside world you'll appear to be my wife in every sense of the word. Only you and I will know it's a business arrangement."

Charli didn't answer. She couldn't. It was too unreal to even contemplate his suggestion. In the awkward, silent moment between them, she began to think about the money he was so casually offering. Her mother was going to need a place to live after the first of the year when her lease expired. For months she had unsuccessfully hunted for an affordable place. If Charli were to move into the Taylor mansion, her mother could have her apartment, and Charli could also pay off the start-up costs of Almost A Wife.

She shook her head. What was *wrong* with her? She was actually considering the absurd idea!

"I'm sorry, but I don't think it would work." Her voice sounded weak and as though it came from far away.

"I think it would, Charli." He leaned forward and gazed into her eyes. "You can trust me. We'll make it all perfectly legal. It's a business arrangement, nothing more. I promise."

"N-nothing more?"

"Separate lives, separate beds. It's all for show, Charli. My bedroom is on the opposite end of the house on the second floor. You don't even have to *see* me if you don't want. Leave some instant oatmeal in a bowl. I'll pour the hot water on myself."

"I'd be a pretty crummy wife, then, wouldn't I?" she joked weakly.

Max grinned in response. "I *would* like breakfast, but I can live without it as long as you'll agree to the other responsibilities."

"But I have other obligations."

"If you'll do this for me, Charli, I'll make it worth your while. Wouldn't you like to be debt free? To hire more employees and to expand your business?"

"You'd do that?"

"It's not going to be an easy job. I entertain and am entertained a lot."

"I'm not afraid of a challenge," Charli retorted, "but I don't like deceiving my friends...."

"A few people will need to know of our arrangement. I understand that. We will simply have to impress upon them the importance of our secret. My friend Walker will know. And my brothers."

"Nita and Richard...."

"And your mother."

She looked at him sharply. How had he known about her mother? A little sleuthing, no doubt. Obviously Taylor was well aware of her financial situation—and knew how tempting his offer might be.

"What about your..." She paused to clear her throat before saying, "Lady friends?"

"I'm not seeing anyone special. I'd rather *not* see anyone for a while. I've told you how I feel. My business is consuming enough right now. If I disappeared from the eligible bachelor list tomorrow, no hearts would be broken."

Charli doubted the truth of that statement. "How long would you want this arrangement to continue?"

"We could try six months for a start. Being a couple has many advantages for me, but if a time comes that one of us sees that our arrangement is no longer practical..." He shrugged, indicating that the dissolution of their partnership would be as easy as a handshake.

Charli was silent for a moment, too stunned to speak. What an absolutely ridiculous suggestion he was making, and yet.... She was more than a little interested. She had struggled all her life. Whatever Charli had, she'd earned by her wits and her hard work. Never having to worry again about making ends meet, about having a large loan looming over her head, was tempting.

Besides, Max's proposal was shaping up to be a very interesting challenge. Whenever in her life someone had told her a task was impossible, it was then that she really began to work. What's more, Charli had never liked forward women anyway. It actually might be rather fun to put one or two aggressive husband-hunters in their places....

Never in her wildest imaginings would Charli have believed she would say she'd consider such an offer, but she heard the words come out of her mouth. "We could try it...."

Max grinned and extended his hand. "I was hoping you'd say that. In the meantime, just treat me like any other client. It'll be a pleasure working with you, Charli."

She mumbled something in return and tried to ignore the uneasiness that nagged at her conscience.

A sharp buzzer rang on the desk console. Taylor pressed a button and Dora's voice drifted into the room.

"Your next client to see you, sir."

Charli quickly gathered her things and stood.

"Give me two minutes." He punched out the secretary's voice. In a silky-smooth tone he said, "Do you have any other questions? If not, I look forward to being almost your husband, Charli McKenna."

"You won't be disappointed. Almost A Wife aims to please." As she retreated toward the door, Charli realized that it was *she* who should be disappointed. She hadn't wanted to do any further business with him, yet here she was agreeing to live a lie with him.

He punched the speaker phone again. "Send Ms. Bolange in."

Charli made a hasty exit, not wanting to meet anyone who might be able to read the display of emotions racing across her features. For better or for worse, she had just agreed to become Max Taylor's wife...almost.

CHAPTER TWO

"UGLY. Garish. Cheap. Gaudy." Charli picked up silk scarves one by one, eyed them critically, passed judgment on each and tossed them back to the counter. "Doesn't anyone make a decent scarf anymore?"

"These are our finest, madame," the clerk fussed, her mouth a worried line. "I assure you that you're the first to be dissatisfied."

"Can you show me something else? Evening bags? Shawls? Anything?"

"This way, madame. We have hand-beaded purses that are simply stunning..."

"What's with you today?" Nita chided as she and Charli followed the worried clerk. "I've never seen you so grumpy! Those scarves were gorgeous."

"Poor workmanship. Weak, insipid colors. They'll never do," Charli growled.

"They would have 'done' for anyone but Max Taylor," Nita said slyly. "Ever since you've been working on his account you've been cranky. What put the burr in your girdle?"

"It just doesn't feel *right* spending all this money on frivolous things." *Or marrying him—almost.*

34

"Since when did you start passing judgment on your client's directives? The gifts are for his employees. If Max had asked you to buy them an assortment of wart removers, you'd do it. That's our business, remember?"

Charli made a sound of disbelief. "I can't believe I took this account. This whole setup is too bizarre!"

"You're the woman who dressed up in a turtle suit and entertained three-year-olds at a birthday party. You're the woman who begged on her hands and knees to get decent caviar for a cocktail party. You're also the woman who said you'd sell your firstborn if the electrician would come to your client's house *before* he started to wire an entire apartment building."

"I didn't really mean that part about my firstborn."

"Even so, Charli, you've done lots crazier things than buying gifts. I don't get it. Why are you so upset?"

Charli looked woefully at the glittering evening bags the clerk was displaying on the counter. "I shouldn't have agreed to take Max Taylor as a client. He asks too much of me."

Nita handled a beaded pearl bag carelessly. "Frankly, I think you like it. You're attracted to Max Taylor and you just won't admit it."

"I'm not attracted to Max!" Charli denied vehemently.

"Then why are you treating him with more care than you do our other clients?"

Charli felt a twinge of guilt at the fact that she hadn't told her assistant about Max's proposal. She knew she'd have to before long; it was only a matter of time before Nita discovered that Charli was moving into the Taylor mansion.

"He could be buying these gifts to burn in his fireplace for all I care!"

"Then why didn't you purchase that scarf? It was perfect."

Charli gave Nita an evil look and slammed her curled fist against the counter. "Oh, all right. I'll take the scarf and the evening bag!" An expression of relief washed over the clerk's face as Charli stomped off, leaving Nita to finish the transaction.

Nita found her slumped in a chair near the three-way mirrors. "Time for lunch? You look like you could use a little resuscitation."

"No time. Max's Christmas list is longer than the census."

"I wonder how I could get on his list," Nita said wistfully. "I could use a few gifts from a good-looking man."

"Not me."

"I don't understand you. There are any number of men who'd be happy to send *you* gifts if you'd give them the least bit of encouragement."

"All I want from men is friendship, nothing more. You know that."

"But they have much more to offer."

Charli closed her eyes as they rode the escalator down to the main floor of the store. "There aren't any bells and whistles with the men I've met. I want to hear bells."

"Bells aren't always a good sign," Nita observed pragmatically. "When I hear bells it usually means there's been a fire or a break-in."

"You know what I mean." Charli stepped off the escalator and eyed the store display before her.

"How about this?" Nita held up a bustier with snappy red garters hanging from the ends of black ribbons. "This would cause bells and whistles. This would be great to bring on a honeymoon!"

A honeymoon. Marriage. Almost.

The image of herself in an outfit like that caused a knot in Charli's stomach. The picture in her mind shimmered there with perfect, blinding clarity. She squeezed her eyes shut and shook her head. "No. I can't."

Nita was staring at her strangely when Charli opened her eyes. "Charli McKenna, you aren't falling for a client, are you?"

Charli gave a resigned sigh. "Nita, we need to talk."

"Something's wrong, isn't it? What's this guy done to you?"

"He wants me to pretend to be his wife."

"His *what*?" Nita's mouth dropped open.

"It's not what you think. He simply needs someone to act as his wife for a number of reasons, mostly professional. It's not anything I wouldn't do through the service. I'll just be working for him exclusively *and pretending that we're married*."

"You actually told him you'd do it?" Nita looked at her in horror.

"Not yet. He's willing to pay more than double what Almost A Wife usually earns, which means I'd be able to pay off those loans I took out on the business."

"Boy, this guy has done a number on you, hasn't he? You, Charli McKenna, are the *last* person to be persuaded to do anything for money even though I know you need it desperately!"

Charli didn't want to admit that his good looks and charm might play any role in her decision. "Look, all I'd be doing is limiting my services to one client and charging him the appropriate rate for it," she said defensively. "Almost A Wife isn't closing. You and Richard would run it as usual."

"So you're telling me that Taylor only wants you to do wifely things for him on a 'professional' basis? That he'll only use your services during the day and your nights and weekends will be your own?"

"Not exactly." She looked away, not wanting to tell her friend that she would be moving into his house.

"Charli, he can't expect you to be at his beck and call twenty-four hours a day, seven days a week."

"He doesn't. But if the need arises, I am willing to work some evenings and weekends. That's why I'm moving into the servants' quarters at his house," she said quietly.

"You're moving in with him?"

"Not yet. If I do move in, it won't be *with* him. It will be *near* him." She emphasized "near."

"You're actually serious about this, aren't you?"

"Look, this could be the perfect arrangement. You know my mother's being evicted from her apartment the first of the year. Mom's had enough trouble in her life. She doesn't need more. With the way rents are in the city, she can't afford much of anything. If I stay at the Taylor estate, Mother can stay in my apartment."

"I don't know, Charli. I think you're getting yourself into something that's going to give you trouble." Nita expressed her concern.

"I know what I'm doing," Charli insisted.

Nita could only gaze at her with doubt in her eyes. "I hope you do, my friend."

"I do," Charli said, although long after they had parted company she was still trying to decide if being Max Taylor's pretend wife was the right decision.

Her apartment seemed cold and barren after the bright lights, familiar music and scent of Christmas potpourri of the department stores. Charli turned on every light and flicked on the gas fireplace. She filled the teakettle with water and set the burner on high just to hear the steaming pot sing. Finally, she opened the packages she'd purchased.

The scarves and evening bags were lovely, she had to admit. Nita had been right. Thoughtfully, Charli picked up the gold foil box she'd brought from the jewelry store. She lifted the lid and plucked out a dangly gold earring. It would be perfect on any one of the women in Max's circle of friends. Elegant, sophisticated, refined.

Charli shuffled to a mirror, held the expensive bauble to her own ear and stared. The gleaming bit of jewelry winked in the waning light and she sighed. It looked ridiculous peeking from beneath the tousled cap of her hair—like a bejeweled tiara on a teenage punk rocker or a feather boa on the mailman. It only highlighted further the contrast between herself and the women who must people Max's world—rich, sophisticated....

She dropped the earring into the box and closed it gently. No matter. The gifts, though completely inappropriate for herself, would please

Max. She flung herself against the davenport, heedless of the packages.

Charli sighed and leaned her head against the couch, wondering if this Christmas would be any different for Max now that he had a wife... almost.

CHAPTER THREE

"ARE you ready?" Max brushed an imaginary
speck of lint from the lapel of his tuxedo and
raised an eyebrow in Charli's direction. "Only
dessert and one speaker left before we can get
out of here."

It was small comfort to Charli to know that
Max felt as miserable as she at the thousand-
dollar-a-plate political fund-raiser they were attending. She brushed her palms across the front
of her rented sequined evening gown and dam-
pened her lower lip with the tip of her tongue.
If political fund-raisers were punishment, she
must have committed a capital crime.

The idea to come was another one of Max's
little "tests." Charli knew perfectly well that he
wanted to see how she handled his social scene
and she would not allow herself to falter.

She was committed to a path now. It felt good
to be doing something for someone else—especially for her mother.

The unfortunate part of all this was that
although Charli could smile gamely and talk
politics with the best of them, thanks to vo-
racious reading and the television news channel,

42

she felt like a fish out of water in this roomful of wealthy, high-society movers and shakers.

Maybe a fish out of water was the wrong analogy, Charli thought grimly as she smiled and took Max's arm. She was a fish, all right. A goldfish. Swimming in a sea of piranhas. The test was to see if she could stay afloat until the night was over....

Charli valued Nita as an assistant for two reasons. First, no matter how crazy the holiday season became, Nita was willing to stay late at the office. Second, she was a good sport. She patiently put up with Charli's offbeat sense of humor.

That was why Charli accepted the mitten job.

"You want me to do *what*?" Nita exclaimed when Charli informed her that the two of them were going to pose as giant mittens.

"Be a mitten." She opened a closet and produced a bright red costume in the shape of a mitten.

"You told me after the turtle gig there'd be no more character acts," Nita protested, eyeing the costume suspiciously. "I don't want to be a mitten—or an overshoe—or a stocking cap."

"It's for a good cause. Mrs. Stanley's senior citizen group is sponsoring a mitten drive for the poor."

"Fine and dandy, but why us? Why mittens?"

"The drop-off point is a huge Christmas tree decorated with mittens, in the IDS center. The sponsors want us to dress as giant mittens and pass out candy snowmen to the children who make a donation." She unzipped the side of the costume. "Try it on."

Nita groaned as she climbed into the metal frame covered with bright red fabric. "Where do my arms go?"

"One stays inside, the other comes out the thumb." Charli adjusted the opening for Nita's face. "How does that feel?"

"Like I'm making a fool of myself." Nita took several steps and twirled around. "Put yours on so I can see what I look like."

Charli complied, waddling around her tiny office in the giant blue mitten.

"Maybe we could do a mitten dance," Nita suggested, wiggling her hips as she hummed a popular rock song.

At the sight of Nita swinging and swaying in her mitten costume, Charli broke into a fit of laughter. Though she tried to steady herself, the cumbersome wool and wire costume upset her equilibrium, causing her to slide to the floor.

Winded and giggly, Nita sank down beside her. "It's a good thing it's after hours. Looking like this, we'd ruin all credibility with our clients."

As if on cue, the door chimed and someone entered the reception area.

"Maybe it's Richard," Nita suggested, struggling unsuccessfully to rise.

Before either could get to her feet, Max strode into Charli's office.

"Ms. McKenna." He stared down at the wriggling human mittens for a seemingly endless moment before he offered Charli a hand.

"Thank you," she said humbly as he helped her to her feet. Nita quickly mitten-waddled away, leaving Charli to face Max alone.

"We're closed," she said, trying not to feel discomfited. It was difficult, considering the predicament—and the costume—she was in.

"Maybe you should bolt the outer door after hours," he suggested with a wry grin. "Especially if you're planning to do something...kinky."

Charli McKenna was the quirkiest, craziest, cutest human being he'd come across in a long time, Max thought as the thumb of Charli's mitten nearly whacked him across the face. Perhaps he should come back when she was dressed like a human being and not an appendage.

She looked very busy. Her desktop was covered with papers, her sewing machine with draping fabric, and both chairs were stacked high with magazines.

She unzipped the mitten and climbed out of the costume. "What brings you to the office?" She self-consciously smoothed the wrinkles out of the oversize knit top she wore over her lace-trimmed leggings.

"Maybe I should come back another time." He looked about her cluttered office. "It's obvious you're busy."

Funny how until he had walked in, she hadn't realized how small her work space was. He seemed to overwhelm the room with his presence, creating an intimacy she found unsettling. She quickly moved one stack of magazines. "It's all right. Please, sit down."

As he eased his tall figure down, Charli pushed aside a pile of papers and boosted herself onto the desktop. "What can I do for you?" She tried to act nonchalant—a difficult challenge considering the way his eyes were glued to her form-hugging leggings.

Max found himself wanting to answer frivolously—to invite her to play and pretend with him, as well. Instead he said, "The time has come, Charli, for you to give me your decision. Are you in or out?"

Charli took a deep breath. "I'm in." There, she had said it. She was committed.

"Then our charade must begin." Max's eyes glittered with pleasure, but his words were all business. "I'm going to give a party next week."

"Next week?" Charli reached for her calendar, glad for an excuse not to meet Max's eyes. "It's rather short notice, but I think I can pull it off. I'll need a guest list . . ."

"Dora can get it for you."

"And menu suggestions..." She hated sounding so breathless.

"Use your own discretion. I'm leaving everything in your hands. Decorations, food, entertainment." For once he could wash his hands of the details. He was surprised at the sense of relief he felt—and the gratitude—to his unlikely business partner.

"Entertainment?"

"I thought perhaps a pianist or a string quartet to provide holiday music."

"Of course." She scribbled frantically on her notepad. "I'll see what's available. It is rather close to the holidays." She paused to think. "What about a tree? A blue spruce would look perfect in your foyer..."

"That won't be necessary. I have an artificial one in the attic."

"Artificial?" She wrinkled her nose.

"There's less mess," he explained. "It's hard to get the tree sap and needles out of the carpet."

"But your house won't be filled with the scent of fresh pine."

Max felt a little guilty at the crestfallen look on her face. He hadn't meant to disappoint Charli with the mention of an artificial tree, but Christmas was just another social opportunity for Taylor Enterprises now. The bleak Christmases with his stepmother as a youth had taken the joy from the holiday long ago.

"What about the trimmings? Are they in the attic, too?"

"I think you'll find an adequate supply at the house. That doesn't mean you can't do something different if you like," he added, surprising himself. "Just make it festive and elegant."

He was amused to see how she perked up after that directive. Charli's emotions were all near the surface and easy to read on her face. It might surprise people, Max mused, if they knew how carefully he watched and judged other people's feelings and emotions. It came in handy in the business world—and in poker.

When Charli had filled in all the necessary details on the client order form, she asked, "Can you think of anything I've missed?"

"Just try to act like a devoted wife, Charli." He almost enjoyed her discomfiture. Apparently she was more comfortable as a mitten than as either a power hostess and/or wife. No matter. She'd do fine. He was a good judge of people.

"Are you sure you want to go through with this?"

"Yes. The timing is perfect. I plan to announce our engagement at the party. There will be enough people there to spread the word. By morning the news will be on the society page."

Words stuck in Charli's throat. "But we haven't known each other very long."

"A romantic, giddy, impulsive thing to do—especially when two people have just met."

"Do you think your friends will even buy that story? I have a hunch you aren't known for being either giddy or impulsive."

"I may be different where love is concerned."

"Oh, Max." Charli pulled at a dark curl. "I don't see how this can work. People are going to wonder why this came up so suddenly."

"I need a reprieve, Charli. I need a rest." His expression turned pensive, even sad. "It's not a pleasant feeling never knowing if people want to know you because you're you or because you're rich and influential. Even if this 'marriage' of ours only lasts a few months, it will give me time to regroup. Besides, we'll tell the truth to the people who really matter to us. What business is it of the rest of the world's anyway? I want a clean cut away from my old personal life. Being a married man should do that quite effectively. Will you help me out?"

"Oh, why not?" Charli sighed. "I do have a reputation for being impulsive."

Max rose to leave. He pulled a check from his suit coat and handed it to her. "This should cover the party expenses."

Max Taylor was spending more on one party than she did for a year's worth of groceries. "I— I'm sure it'll be sufficient," she answered, eyes widening.

He turned toward the door, engaged with a mental battle with himself. He looked at the mitten costume on the floor, then at Charli's funky leggings. "And one last thing, Ms. McKenna. Consider a dress for the occasion a part of your expense report."

He hated himself even as he said it. He liked her Peter Pan approach to dressing, but it simply wasn't suitable for the group he planned to entertain. Rather than risk her making a mistake, he'd had to say it.

"That isn't necessary." Charli rubbed her hands on her thighs, suddenly feeling very small and bare as he looked up and down her petite figure. Though Max's gaze *seemed* impersonal, Charli felt undressed when he was through.

The disconcerting part was that she rather liked it. Max had incredible eyes. As his gaze rested on her, Charli felt her skin warm and glow, a totally unacceptable response to a client—especially in these circumstances.

"I have formal clothes," she said with a lift of her chin, wishing her top didn't have tumbling teddy bears splattered all over it.

"I'm sure you do, but since I'm hiring you to be my hostess—er, fiancée, you'll purchase an appropriate dress, I presume."

"Oh, I'll purchase a dress, all right," Charli mumbled to herself as soon as Max departed. "Wait until Mr. Big Shot Taylor sees what Charli McKenna can do when she puts her mind to it."

"Did you say something to me?" Nita asked, poking her head into Charli's office.

"Uh-uh. I was just thinking out loud," Charli retorted. "And thanks for deserting me just now."

"I thought you might like a few moments alone with your sweetie," Nita said to justify her absence.

"He's *not* my 'sweetie.' It's business!" Charli retorted.

"Well, you're the one he wants to do business with."

"Yeah, business, business, business." Charli shoved aside the image of a chic cocktail dress and dangling diamond earrings. She would do well to remember that dressing in fancy clothes for Max Taylor's pleasure would always be business. Just business.

"What do you think? Is she centered?" Richard Hughes asked Charli from his perch on the stepladder.

"She's a little tipped to the left," Charli answered, eyeballing the angel atop the artificial Christmas tree in Max's foyer.

Richard carefully adjusted her wings.

"That's it. Perfect." Charli stood back to admire the tree trimmed in gold. "What do you think? Is it a tree any corporate executive would envy?"

"A tree's a tree, Charli," Richard said, climbing down from the ladder.

"But don't you think the gold bulbs I purchased look better than all those ugly blue things we found in the attic?"

"I think you're worrying too much about what this guy's gonna think about his tree."

"He's my best client. He spent more on this party than I do for a whole year of groceries. I can't afford not to worry." She fussed with a strand of gold beads dangling from the tree. "I'm not sure I should have added these ropes of gold."

"It looks exactly like the picture you showed me in that high-society magazine," he said with a note of exasperation. "The whole house does. It looks so good you could film one of those Christmas TV specials here."

"We did do a good job, didn't we?" A smile of satisfaction graced Charli's face as she wandered through the house.

"Does this mean I can put the ladder away?" Richard asked, trailing along behind her.

"Go ahead. I've one last item to hang, but I'll use the step stool from the kitchen."

While Richard returned the ladder to the basement, Charli hung mistletoe in the entrance to the dining room. She had just finished and was about to carry the step stool back to the kitchen when a pair of arms circled her waist.

"I'll put that away for you," Richard offered, relieving her of the step stool. Gently he pulled her under the mistletoe. "No man in his right

mind would pass up this opportunity, Charli,''
he teased before pressing his lips to hers.

If Charli hadn't been so tired, she might have
tried to avoid the kiss. She liked having Richard
as an employee and didn't want to complicate
her life by letting romance enter into their relationship. Besides, she could hardly be seen
dating while she was "engaged" to Max. But it
was the Christmas season. What harm could there
be in an innocent kiss beneath mistletoe?

None at all, if Max hadn't walked in at the
precise moment when her lips met Richard's.
Startled, she tried to push out of Richard's arms.

"Let me go!'' she whispered through clenched
teeth, a blush firing her cheeks.

"Relax! I thought you said this marriage thing
was a sham!'' he grumbled, releasing her.

Free, she turned to Max. "We just finished.
How do you like it?'' She gestured toward the
decorated foyer and the tree trimmed in gold.

"It's satisfactory.''

"Only 'satisfactory'?'' Richard appeared ready
to speak his mind.

Charli quickly sent him to get their coats from
the other room.

"I'm paying you to decorate my house, Charli,
not use it for a romantic liaison,'' Max muttered
coldly when Richard was gone.

"Richard works for me.''

"Hardly someone you should be kissing under
the mistletoe, then. What if someone other than

myself had walked in? How would it look to have my fiancée kissing the hired help? Charli, every good business person knows you don't mix business with pleasure.''

''I'll keep that in mind,'' she answered glibly.

The night of Max's party Charli often needed to remind herself that it was her business, not good fortune, that was responsible for her being the hostess of such a gala affair.

What's more, Max was acting as though she were someone extraordinary in his life. Her overnight bag was in the guest room. Max hovered over her like a solicitous lover. He'd even sent her flowers to wear in her hair. She could almost believe—if she pressed reality into the farthest reaches of her mind—that he did take pride—and pleasure—in her presence.

Did her royal treatment have anything to do with the dress?

It had felt magical since the moment Charli had slipped it on in the department store—an upscale, sophisticated, Cinderella dress. It was black velvet, off-the-shoulder, body-molding dynamite meant to blow away a man's poise and veneer of control. So far it had worked like a charm. Max hadn't even dared to order her around the kitchen earlier. It had obviously taken all his willpower to keep his eyes on her face and not the gently rounded slope of her breasts or the alabaster whiteness of her naked shoulder. Charli grinned inwardly. It had felt wonderful to stuff her leggings and oversize sweatshirt in the closet tonight and—presto!—have a princess emerge.

Too bad Princess Charli had to worry about the canapes and crudités. It would have been more fun to have Max drinking champagne from her slipper.

"Speaking of slippers," Charli muttered. "Where are mine?"

"Under the table, madame," the white-hatted chef said with a sneer of disapproval. An artiste, he didn't like sharing his space with Charli or the waiters. Tough, Charli thought to herself. All the chef had to do was cook up a gourmet buffet table for fifty that would knock the socks off these wealthy, jaded, overfed friends of Max's. *She* had to make sure nothing went wrong—and play the biggest, most important role of her life to boot.

While Charli was attempting to ease into her unfamiliar role as lady of the house, Max was in the living room dodging female attention. Charli watched as a lovely brunette with shapely legs and an impressive cleavage cast doelike adoring glances Max's way. In response, Max swilled a glass of champagne and fixed a glazed expression on his features.

"That will end soon, I hope," Charli muttered.

She glided discreetly toward a table where a champagne punch was flowing from a tiered crystal fountain. Waiters in penguin suits with crisp linen towels draped over their arms were serving the ambrosial nectar with great ceremony.

From the punch table, Charli moved toward the buffet. There was still plenty of caviar and toast points, stuffed mushrooms and miniature pastry puffs filled with chicken. Soon it would be time to bring out the wild rice soup, lobster bisque and array of exotic breads, meats and cheeses.

Max, meanwhile, was across the room, deep in conversation with a wizened-looking old gentleman in a conservative navy suit.

"Nice party, Taylor."

"Thank you, Mr. Emmett. Glad you could come."

"I usually avoid these things. Frivolous. Too much champagne and too little roast beef, if you know what I mean."

Max smiled to himself and chalked up a point for Charli. She'd put together exactly the type of get-together that appealed to Franklin Emmett— elegant, proper, stylish, and yet with a distinctive flair, much like old Emmett himself. Max had wished for years to be one of Emmett's "chosen few," those prestigious stockholders who sat on the board of his company, but, though Emmett genuinely seemed to like and to trust Max, the invitation had never come. Something, Max didn't know what, stood in the way. Maybe tonight a corner had been turned....

"Try the smoked salmon," Max encouraged. "Charli said it was the best she'd ever found."

"Charli? So that's her name." Emmett's clownish little face pucked with pleasure. "I've been waiting for you to find a woman, Taylor. I hope you're serious about her. It's time you settled down."

"Pardon me, sir?"

"Settled down. You know, quit playing the field. That Charli doesn't look like the type of woman who'd stand for it and I'm glad. I never knew what you saw in the string of women you always had pursuing you. It's flattering, I suppose, but not very good for the image."

"Image?" Max was beginning to sound like a puzzled echo.

"That's something I always watch for when picking my board of directors. My company has always had a reputation for promotion of sound family values. I want my board of directors to be a showcase for such. Thought you'd realized that years ago, Taylor."

Max gave Emmett an enigmatic smile. "Then I think you'll be very pleased as the evening goes on, sir."

Emmett raised one grizzled eyebrow. A smile played at the corner of his lip. "Really? I always like an event with a little suspense. Now I think I'll have some of that smoked salmon you recommended."

As Emmett strolled off, Walker came up behind Max and smacked him hard on the shoulder. "Interesting conversation, Max?"

"*Verrrrry* interesting. I finally know what's kept me off Emmett's board all these years."

"What's that?"

"'Family values.' That's been the barrier. I thought I was overlooked because he didn't believe I could bring enough expertise to the board to benefit him, but all this time he just didn't approve of my dating habits!"

"He told you that?"

"Yes, and that bit of information is worth its weight in gold, Walker," Max continued, "both literally and figuratively. It's the key to what I've dreamed about. I'll have double the power and prestige with a foot in the door to Emmett's business as well as mine. And I've got the key to all of that here tonight."

"I don't get it, Max. What are you talking about?"

"Charli, of course! I hired her to get out of the social rat race, but a position on Emmett's board is worth putting a real ring on her finger, don't you think?"

Walker glared at Max. "Aren't you enjoying this a little too much? If you carry it any further, you'll be hiring child actors to be your 'children.'"

"Some of the most influential people in this country sit on Emmett's board, Walker. I could be one of them. I hate to say it, but sometimes I think I'd do *anything* to sit on the board of Emmett's company..." He glanced up and saw Charli walking toward them. "What is it?"

"My jacket. I think I left my lipstick there."

Max dug into the inside pocket of his suit and withdrew a tube. "You gave it to me."

"Oh, well, thanks." Charli took the tube, still warm from the heat of his body, and turned away. Two emotions were surging through her. The first was curiosity. Who was this man Emmett, and why did Max want so badly to impress him? And why did the idea that her lipstick had been riding around next to Max's heart all evening make her feel slightly breathless. Already they were sharing little intimacies that husbands and wives shared all the time. Could she ignore them and the feelings they aroused in her?

Charli was on her way toward the dessert table when a portly gentleman grabbed her by the arm and reeled her toward himself. He addressed Max with a hearty, "You got yourself a real gem, Max! This is the finest party you've ever given. When did you find her?"

Max was cool, smooth and suave in his black tuxedo. "It's a secret, Anton. Charli is mine."

Anton eyed Charli appreciatively. "And what Max wants, Max gets." Then, remembering his manners, the older man added, "Truly, this is a lovely party and you are an exquisite hostess. My most sincere compliments."

Charli forced her sweetest smile. She needed to talk to the harpist about her selection of music. The Christmas tree ice sculpture was melting far too quickly and the miniature cheesecakes appeared a little burned. She didn't have time to watch Max preen his feathers because *she* could put on a good party.

"You're too kind. Now, if you'll excuse me, I see some details that need tending to. Can I get you more champagne? A truffle? Espresso, perhaps?"

Before she could leave, Max grabbed her by the wrist. "Wait. I think it's time we made our announcement." He turned to the harpist and gave a nod. Strains of "The Wedding March" filled the room, catching the attention of all the guests.

Smiling, Max lifted a glass of champagne. "I've been waiting all evening to make a very important announcement." He slipped his arm around Charli's waist and said, "I feel very privileged to say that this lovely woman at my side is now my wife. We were married earlier today in a private ceremony."

A gasp of surprise and a round of applause echoed throughout the room, with good cheer and toasts floating on the air. No one noticed that the bride seemed as shocked as the other guests in the room.

Charli didn't hear the cheers, for Max's lips were descending upon hers in so intimate a kiss that it left her unable to think about anything but this man who had told the world they were married. What had happened to their "engagement"?

Although it lasted but a few seconds, to Charli the kiss seemed to go on for a lifetime, leaving her breathless and painfully aware that Max was indeed dangerous to her heart.

"What did you do that for? I thought we were going to announce our engagement," she whispered. "I'm not ready to be married!"

"Believe me, it's much better this way," he said reassuringly.

"Better for whom? How are we going to fool anybody when we aren't living together?"

"That's easily changed."

Charli's stomach flip-flopped at the thought. "What about my family, my friends?"

"You can tell them, Charli, but be careful, so you don't spoil the charade."

Further conversation was impossible as they were besieged with congratulations. As soon as the turmoil died down, she slipped away, leaving Max to entertain his friends. She ducked behind a fluted column for a moment to close her eyes and gather her thoughts. It didn't really matter, she supposed, whether they were "engaged" or "married." Sooner or later she would have to pretend to be his wife. She only wished she'd had a chance to tell her mother first. Charli gave a weary sigh.

"You're doing great. Relax."

"Walker!" She'd met Max's friend Walker Calhoun early in the evening. Walker was a wildlife photographer, laid-back and pleasant.

"Listen—" Walker took Charli by the elbow "—you look a bit frazzled. Since I'm Max's best friend and he practically gave this party with me in mind, I think you should come with me and sit down for a minute."

Charli gave him a squinty stare as he steered her toward the bedroom. Walker laughed. "I'm not putting a move on you, Charli, although I must say it's a great line. Five minutes' rest will do you good." He opened the door for her to enter.

She couldn't deny that. She hadn't eaten all day. Her feet hurt. The chef was a royal pain in the neck. The party was moving nicely without her. Did she dare take a break?

"Just for a minute, then," she finally conceded.

"Two minutes." Walker plucked a glass of champagne off the serving tray being passed before following her. Charli sank into one of two wing chairs flanking the fireplace and he sat down across from her.

"To you, Charli. To your new marriage and to a great party." He lifted his glass in salute.

"Thanks." She smiled, acknowledging the toast. "But some of the credit should go to Max."

Walker chuckled. "You're right. He *bought* a good hostess...and wife, almost."

Charli sipped her champagne thoughtfully. "So you know. You sound as though you don't approve."

"Max is a smart man and a good one. His style is different from mine, but I've learned not to second-guess him. He's usually right."

"How long have you known him?"

"Many, many years. I love Max like a brother."

"Tell me about him," Charli said impulsively. "What was it like being ten years old with Max?"

Walker leaned back in his chair and fingered the stem of his glass thoughtfully. "Max was never a child, not really. He had to grow up quickly. His mother died when he was very young. His father remarried, but his stepmother was..." Walker grew cautious. "Never too crazy about Max or his little brothers. She liked possessions more than she liked people. For as long as I can remember, Max has tried to be both mother and father for those boys."

Walker's expression turned pensive. "My own mother is the one who encouraged me to become a wildlife photographer. She nurtured my eye for beauty." He shrugged. "Maybe Max would have been more content, less restless, if he'd had a mother like mine. He certainly wouldn't have had to struggle so hard to make up for what he lacked as a child."

Charli was riddled with curiosity. There were a million questions she wanted to ask to uncover this new, surprising side of her Max.

"So there you are!" Max surged into the room. "The chef has a question about the buffet table and the champagne is running low. Besides, my guests want to congratulate my new wife."

Charli scrambled out of her chair. "Why not? I'm in too deep to get out now anyway. I'd better get back to the party. I only meant to rest a moment. I'll take care of the chef right away."

She moved toward the door, leaving Max and Walker behind. Their soft, private words didn't follow her.

"I saw old Emmett making his way toward you after the announcement," Walker observed. "What did he want?"

"To drop a bomb on my head. He asked me to be on his board."

"Just like that?" Walker snapped his fingers.

"He said he had a spot and he's been waiting for just the right man. He was dead serious about that 'family values' thing. Until I made the announcement tonight, he felt he couldn't ask me because I didn't really represent the image of the company. Now he's handing it to me on a gold platter."

"But he thinks you're *really* married!"

"And I won't tell him differently unless he asks."

"Is this going to work, Max?"

"Why not? Charli's beautiful, talented, charming, a wonderful hostess...."

"You know what I mean! What if you meet someone and want to...you know...date?"

"I'm on vacation from that, Walker. I've been burned every time I've put my hand near the fire. Charli and I have a deal worked out that will make us both very happy. Don't worry. Everything is working out even better than I'd dreamed."

Charli returned to the bedroom in search of a missing earring just in time to hear Walker inquire, "What if you fall in love with her?"

"With Charli? Whatever made you say that, Walker?"

"Maybe she could be the kind of woman you'd like to get under the mistletoe. Are you going to deny such thoughts haven't crossed your mind?"

Charli didn't wait for Max's response. She escaped to the kitchen where she managed to keep herself occupied for the rest of the evening.

She and Max were digging themselves deeper and deeper into this marriage sham. What's more, Walker Calhoun's words stung in her brain. Was his intuition savvy? *Could* she be the kind of woman Max would like under his mistletoe?

It was 3:00 a.m. before the final guest departed. Fortunately the caterers had cleaned up and vanished after the final call for the midnight buffet.

That left Charli emptying ashtrays and carrying scattered crystal goblets to the kitchen.

She was debating the fate of the crab dip when Max padded into the kitchen, his shirt open to the waist, his tie dangling off to one side, a drink in his hand. It was a shockingly pleasant sight. Her mouth went dry.

"How do you feel about leftover crab dip for breakfast?" she asked.

Max skewered a stray shrimp on the stirrer from his glass. "I hate crab dip—any time of day. Should you be cleaning up in that dress?" He moved closer to her and Charli felt her breathing accelerate. She was forced to remind herself that business with Max should involve no pleasure, particularly pleasure this giddy and sensuous.

Her hand shook as she dumped the remains of the dip down the garbage disposal. "Everything else will refrigerate nicely. Frankly, there's not much left over."

"You were magnificent tonight, Charli. Best party I've ever given. They all said so." There was an odd inflection in his voice.

"Even Walker?"

"Forget Walker. He's a terminal windbag." Although the rebuff was gruffly spoken, there was affection underlying his words.

"He said you were best friends," she said softly.

Max wobbled his head. "True. But that doesn't mean you should believe everything he said."

Charli pulled out a bar stool and shimmied onto it. "I found him to be rather... charming."

"Perhaps. In a reptilian sort of way."

Charli burst into laughter. "Quit teasing!"

Max grinned then, a wide, relaxed smile that took ten years from his features and made him movie-star handsome. "Let's not talk about Walker anymore." He seemed dead-set on avoiding any conversation which might somehow accidently allow him to reveal something of himself. That obviously included conversation about his friendship with Walker Calhoun.

It was difficult not to like Max when he was in this mood, Charli mused. He padded softly around the kitchen stocking-footed, touching a crystal decanter here, a bud vase there.

"I didn't realize I owned so many things that could be used for a party," he commented.

"You don't. Most of it's rented and will be returned tomorrow."

He chuckled pleasantly. "You're a magician. Do you know that?" He settled across from her and took the fingers of her left hand in his own. "It was a wonderful party. Thank you."

Charli felt zingers of sensation bolting up and down her arm. "Almost A Wife aims to please." She wanted to pull away, but her defenses had melted. Mesmerized, she watched him knead the palm of her hand with his thumb. The tension which had sparked between them all evening exploded.

Suddenly, a gleeful, impish expression slid across his features. He patted the pocket of his trousers before drawing out a tiny, bedraggled sprig of mistletoe.

"I believe there's one small kiss left in this poor little plant," he murmured, holding it above her head, grabbing her hand with his free one. Before Charli could stop him, he leaned over and brushed his lips across hers.

Stunned, she was rooted to the spot, her senses aflame, her lips longing for more. The dusky aroma of his after-shave lingered, as did the dry warmth of his mouth.

If a tattered sprig of mistletoe could wreak so much havoc, it was a good thing there wasn't an entire bush in sight.

"Oh, by the way, I almost forgot!" He released her hand to reach beneath the counter and grab an exquisitely wrapped foil box. "This is for you. A thank-you gift."

Charli stared at the box for a long moment. A coil of tension twisted around her insides until she felt an almost physical pain. She recognized the holiday foil paper. Nita had wrapped this box.

"Open it."

Woodenly, Charli reached for the box.

It was a gold pen and pencil set, engraved with the words "Charli M—Better Than A Wife."

She fought to control the bitter sensations swirling within her. "Thank you."

"You're welcome."

Charli chomped down hard on her lower lip, trying to rein in the words threatening to spill out. Try as she might, she failed. "Who bought this for you? Your secretary?"

His reaction was as physical as if he'd been slapped. "A very...feline...response, Ms. McKenna. I'd expected better of you."

"Sorry, but I've purchased so many gifts for you I was surprised that my own name wasn't on the list." She hated herself even as she spoke. She sounded so small and spiteful, yet for some reason she was hurt, hurt and insulted. What had seemed so personal and so beautiful had once again become strictly business.

Max drew himself to his full height, the relaxed camaraderie gone. "I apologize if I hurt your feelings, Charli. But you, of all people, should understand. You make it your business to buy gifts that others will give. Isn't it a bit hypocritical to expect every gift given to you to be chosen with strict personal attention?"

"Maybe, for a moment, I was swept up in this fantasy we're creating. Don't worry, I won't forget again."

"Good. I expect you to move into the house tomorrow."

"You expect a lot of things, don't you, Max?" Charli quipped. "You haven't been playing by the rules of our game. Why should I?"

"Because I am the one paying for this little game." Max lifted his glass in mock tribute to their sham of a marriage.

Head held high, Charli marched out of the kitchen. She wanted to get far away from Max on this, the first night of their new life.

CHAPTER FOUR

"Is it too early to offer my congratulations again?" Franklin Emmett poked his head inside Max's office.

"Franklin, come in." Max rose to greet him.

"Forgive me for barging in like this, but I wanted to talk to you before you and Charli left for the holidays."

Max shot him a puzzled look.

"In Big Sky. You *are* spending the Christmas holiday there, aren't you?"

"Yes, I am, but..."

"Splendid. I can't wait for my wife Barbara to meet Charli."

"You're going to Montana for the holidays?" Max's voice turned cautious.

"Yes. I took your advice and invested in a place just down the road from yours. That means we're bound to run into each other at the lodge. We'll have to get together for a little Christmas cheer."

"I'm sure you'll be busy with your grandchildren," Max hedged. "There's no need to do business over the holidays. You should be with your family."

71

Franklin waved a hand. "They'll be out skiing most of the time. This is a wonderful opportunity for us married men to spend some time with our wives."

Max smiled weakly. "I'd like Charli to meet your wife, too." He realized that his little game of pretend had the potential to become quite complicated.

As soon as Franklin had gone, Max grabbed his coat and headed for her office.

"Some woman named Dora called to tell you Max is on his way over," Nita announced as Charli picked up her phone messages.

Charli groaned. "I hope he's not coming to do some macho number on me and drag me off to his castle."

"Uh-oh. Sounds like the honeymoon is over."

Charli's shoulders stiffened. "There was no honeymoon, as you well know."

"So what's the problem?"

Charli sighed. "He ordered me to pack my things and move in before the weekend was over."

"Did you?"

"No, I did not!"

"Why not? I thought that was part of your agreement."

"It is, but I'm not going to let him treat me like a real wife. He wasn't even supposed to announce our 'marriage' last night. I'd thought that was coming later. He can't treat me this way. I'm his business partner, not his slave. The least he could have done was ask me if it was convenient for me to move in."

Nita eyed her curiously. "And then you would have done it?"

"Maybe...oh, I don't know. I wish he'd just leave me be for five minutes. The man has more chores to take care of than..."

She stopped in mid-sentence as the door was flung open and Max stormed in. "We need to talk," he said, heading for her office.

Charli could only trail after him, flinging Nita an "I told you so" look.

Max handed Charli the newspaper. "We made the news, page 7C."

She found the society column and frowned. "They make it sound so..."

"Unbelievable?" Max supplied.

"I was going to say expedient. Everyone's going to think I'm expecting a baby."

"We should be pleased. We've convinced people it's a real marriage. That is what we wanted. But this isn't the reason I came to see you."

"If you've come to see why I haven't moved in, it's because I'm not ready." She immediately took the offensive. "I need a few days to pack."

"Very well."

She looked at him oddly. "You don't mind?"

"Would it matter to you if I did?"

She blushed, much to her chagrin. "I'll have my things together by the end of the week."

"That's fine."

His sudden acquiescence made her feel vulnerable. "So if you didn't come all the way over here to discuss our living arrangements, why did you come?"

"Do you ski, Charli?"

"Sorry. Is that something Mrs. Maxwell Taylor needs to know how to do?"

"It might make things a bit more fun for you."

"What things?" she asked suspiciously.

"Like our holiday in Big Sky."

"Big Sky, Montana?" Her jaw dropped.

"I have a condominium there. It's where my family spends every Christmas. My brothers and their wives all go for the holiday. This year with all the snow it's bound to be an excellent ski season."

"I'm sure you'll have a good time. If you leave me a list of things to do, I'll see that they're taken care of by the time you return."

"I don't think you understand."

Charli had a sinking feeling in the pit of her stomach.

"I need you to be with me in Montana."

She could only stare at him in stunned disbelief. "You don't really expect me to spend Christmas at a ski resort?" she finally asked.

"Oh, but I do. We're supposed to be newlyweds, Charli. How's it going to look if we spend our first Christmas apart?"

"You never told me there would be traveling involved with this job."

"All of your expenses will be paid."

"It doesn't matter. I can't do it."

"You have to do it."

She stood with her hands on her hips and faced him squarely. "Christmas is a time to be with family. I'm not going to spend it with strangers at some playground for the rich."

"Big Sky is hardly that."

"It doesn't matter. I'm not going."

"I'll give you a bonus."

"No."

He named an exorbitant amount of money that caused Charli's eyes to widen. She thought about the phone calls her mother had been plagued with from irate bill collectors. With the bonus Max was willing to pay her, she could at least buy her mother a respite from the creditors who had been harassing her ever since Charli's stepfather had lost his job.

"All right. I'll do it." Charli thought she saw a flicker of satisfaction in Max's eyes, but it was quickly replaced by an indifference that sent a chill down her spine.

He scribbled something on a notepad, then tore off the paper and handed it to her. "Call Dora and she'll get you a plane ticket. Here's the phone number to the resort complex. If you call ahead they'll make sure the condo is stocked with groceries.''

''Groceries? Do you expect me to cook?''

''My sister-in-law enjoys being in the kitchen.''

''Then what will my responsibilities be?''

''We'll work that out on the plane.'' He started to leave, then stopped himself. ''One last thing. Go over to the White Wolf and pick out whatever clothing you need. I've made arrangements for everything to be charged to my account.''

''That won't be necessary.'' Charli's shoulders stiffened with pride. ''I told you, I don't ski.''

''You'll still need appropriate clothing.''

What did he think? That she didn't have enough sense to wear warm clothes? ''I do have a winter jacket and boots,'' she said pointedly.

''I know you do, but if you're going to pretend to be my wife, you need to look the part,'' he reminded her.

''All right. I'll go to the White Wolf and buy the expensive clothing befitting Mrs. Max Taylor,'' she said churlishly.

Again, there was a brief flicker of satisfaction in Max's eyes. ''Most women would jump at the chance to spend a man's money,'' he said as he turned to leave.

''I'm not most women,'' Charli told him, lifting her chin.

''No, I'm discovering you most certainly are not.''

Charli couldn't read the expression in his eyes, but she thought she saw admiration. And that made her heart beat a little faster.

After Max left, Charli had another visitor storm through the front door—her mother. Charli winced. She knew what was coming.

"Charlene Katherine McKenna! What is the meaning of this?" She waved a newspaper in the air.

"I can explain," Charli said evenly, pushing her mother down onto one of the upholstered chairs. "Calm down."

"How can I be calm when I learn of my only daughter's marriage from my next door neighbor who saw it in the newspaper? I thought you said you were only going to pretend to be his fiancée!"

"I'm not married," Charli said slowly.

"You're not the Charli McKenna listed here?" Ruth McKenna O'Connor pointed a finger at the society column.

"Yes, I am, but . . ." She sat down across from her mother and lifted her calloused hands into her own.

"I'm pretending to be Max Taylor's wife now, that's all. I'm simply doing a job . . . a job I'm getting paid a lot of money to do."

"Well, that's all fine and dandy, but in the meantime the rest of the world thinks you're married to this fellow."

"The people who are close to me will know the truth. That's all that's important." Charli could see the disapproval on her mother's lined face. "It's just a job, Mother."

"Are you sure Maxwell Taylor understands that?"

"Yes. We have an agreement. It's business. That's all," she assured her, as the kiss Max had given her the night of the party flashed in her memory. "I'm glad you're here, because I have to talk to you about Christmas."

"I suppose you're going to tell me you're bringing this pretend husband to dinner?"

"I'm afraid I'm not going to be able to spend Christmas with you and Bill. I have to work."

Her mother's face fell. "Oh, Charli," she said with a moan.

"Mr. Taylor spends his holiday in Montana. I don't want to go, but if I do, he'll give me a huge bonus. I'll be able to help you and Bill get back on your feet."

"I don't want you making that kind of sacrifice just to pay off my bills," her mother protested. "It won't be Christmas if we're not together."

Charli was torn between wanting to help her mother yet not wanting to disappoint her. "We can have our own celebration when I get home."

Her mother wore a skeptical look.

"Please say you understand, Mother."

"I'm not sure I do, Charli. After what happened with Griffith, I can't comprehend why you would want anything to do with a man whose name is on the society pages."

"I'm not going to get involved emotionally with Max Taylor. I simply work for him."

"Charli, you can't live with a man, feign a marriage, and not get involved with him emotionally," her mother warned.

"We're going to be in separate wings of a gigantic house. Besides, Max Taylor is not my type."

"But what if you're *his* type? What happens then?"

"He could have any number of wealthy, society women. He doesn't want someone who shops at garage sales."

Her mother sighed. "I think this job is a mistake, Charli, but I can see by that stubborn tilt of your chin that you're not going to listen to anything I have to say."

Charli gave her mother's shoulder a squeeze. "Everything's going to work out just fine. In six months time I'll own Almost A Wife lock, stock, and barrel, you and Bill will be out of debt, and this whole charade will be over. Trust me."

"I do trust you. It's this rich man I don't trust," her mother said, her brow wrinkling.

"You don't need to worry. There's not a rich man alive who's going to have the chance to break my heart ever again."

* * *

A white, stretch limousine carried Charli and all of the luggage to the airport. As Max had instructed, she had purchased enough clothing for their stay in Montana. Among those purchases was a *faux* fur-trimmed, lemon-yellow ski parka which she now wore with a pair of matching stretch pants.

Not one to wallow in self-pity, Charli had made up her mind to enjoy her paid vacation in Big Sky, even if it did mean she would be away from home at Christmas. Having moved often as a child, she knew that certain situations demanded that you make the most of them.

This was one of those situations. She didn't want to spend Christmas with Max and his family, but all the wishes in the world wouldn't change anything. She would pretend to be a wife and forget what might have been back home.

"Flight 634 will be leaving from Gate 27 on the gold concourse, Mrs. Taylor," the airline representative informed her as she checked her luggage at the ticket counter. "I believe your husband has already checked in."

Mrs. Taylor. Your husband. Charli wasn't accustomed to being called anyone's wife. Even though she and Max were living in the same house, she felt like one of the servants, seeing little of him except when he had errands for her to run.

That's why his attentiveness on their flight caught her off guard. He played his role as a newlywed very well, staying close to her side, touching her affectionately and smiling lovingly as if he truly were her new husband.

Charli rather enjoyed his attention. As much as she hated to admit it, she felt rather special sipping champagne in the first-class section of the airplane with a handsome man at her side.

Not once in the period she had dated Griffith had he treated her as if she were first-class. The only time they had ever traveled together they had sat in economy and never would he have put her needs ahead of his—which was exactly what Max had done ever since she had arrived at the departure gate.

If Charli could have imagined the perfect getaway in the mountains, Max's condominium was it. Nestled in the trees, it had a view of the Rockies that took her breath away. Vaulted beamed ceilings and tall windows brought the brightness of the winter snow indoors. Richly paneled walls provided a lodgelike atmosphere that called for a fire to be built in the massive stone fireplace.

"Cozy" was how Charli described it. When Max deposited her suitcases in the bedroom that was right next door to his, she began to have her doubts as to the wisdom of the trip.

"I'm sorry there's not a private bath with this room," he told her.

"It doesn't matter."

"You might not say that once my family gets here," he said with a wry grin.

"When are the others coming?"

"Tomorrow morning. I always come a day early to get everything ready."

"I see." She glanced about nervously.

There was a long silence between them. "Charli," he finally said, "you've been living in my house for the past two weeks. You should know by now you can trust me to behave like a gentleman."

"The thought hadn't crossed my mind that you would behave any other way," she lied.

"Good." He glanced at his watch. "Take some time to get settled, then we'll have dinner at the lodge."

Charli nodded, although she thought it would be better if she kept to herself as much as possible for the next few days, or at least until Max's brothers arrived. There was something seductive about the way she was treated when people regarded her as Max Taylor's wife. It would be wise not to let that false emotion get in the way of business.

"Business, this is business," Charli repeated to herself as she put her clothes away in the pine chest of drawers.

She tucked her lacy lingerie beneath a heavy wool sweater. It felt too odd leaving it on top where a drawer ajar might reveal something so intimate and personal.

*   *   *

Ever since he had seen Charli arrive at the airport looking like a delightful yellow bumblebee, Max had been fighting the urge to treat her like a woman instead of a business partner. It hadn't helped that she had smelled like a flower garden, either.

On the airplane she had been nothing but a distraction to him. A lot of good it had done to bring his laptop computer when the only place his eyes had wanted to be was on her elfin figure.

Max still didn't know what it was about her that attracted him so. She was nothing at all like the women he usually dated. And she had certainly made it clear that she had no interest in him other than as someone to give her a paycheck.

He had seen the look of apprehension that had flickered in her eyes when she had discovered his brothers weren't coming until tomorrow. Until they had been standing in her bedroom, he hadn't given much thought to the fact that the two of them would be alone. Now it was all he could think about.

That was why he had taken her to dinner at the lodge. It would be much easier to keep conversation on a business level with other people around. Max was almost relieved to see Franklin and Barbara Emmett waving them to their table. Barbara's chatter and Franklin's war stories would keep their minds off each other.

What Max hadn't counted on was Charli's form-hugging stretch pants and clingy sweater. It was enough to destroy a man's peace of mind. If she had looked like a bumblebee earlier in the day, she now looked like a butterfly. The sweater was a sparkly rainbow of glittery purple and pink.

From the moment he had first seen her he had wanted to compliment her on it, but had avoided putting the conversation on a personal level. Finally, as they left the dining room and headed toward the coat check, he asked, "Did you get that outfit at the White Wolf?"

"Yes. Why? Is there something wrong with it?"

"No. It suits you."

"Thank you," she said stiffly. Suddenly the sound of country-western music came from the lounge. "You didn't tell me they had a country bar here," she said in an accusing voice.

"I didn't know you were interested."

She looked longingly toward the lounge. "I love country." And before Max knew it, she was standing in the doorway to the lounge, tapping her foot to the rhythm of the music, waving him over.

"It's late," Max said pointedly as he joined her in the lounge, carrying both of their coats.

"Can't we stay for a little bit?" she pleaded. "It's been ages since I've been line dancing."

The bar was already filled to overflowing, with standing room only. Before Max had a chance to say another word, Charli was on the dance floor between two men who were stomping their cowboy boots to the country beat.

As one song led into another, Max watched in amazement as Charli did all the intricate steps of the various line dances. Her cheeks were flushed, her eyes sparkling as she moved in synchronization with the other dancers. When the band finally slowed the tempo with a country ballad, one of the men in cowboy boots asked Charli to dance.

Max intervened. "Excuse me, but the lady is leaving," he said to the surprised cowboy. When Charli shot him a look of outrage, he whispered close to her ear, "You're supposed to be my wife, a role you apparently forget when you hear honky-tonk music."

Charli didn't say a word, but allowed Max to pull her by the hand as if she were a recalcitrant child.

"I'm sorry," she said as they walked out into the cold, brisk night. "Sometimes I get a little carried away by music. I forgot that we're here on business."

"I'd appreciate it if you worked hard at remembering that is the *only* reason you're here," Max said, as much for *his* benefit as for hers.

"Does that mean I'm not entitled to have any fun?" she asked saucily as they followed the plowed walkway back to the condo.

"As long as it's not at my expense."

"I wasn't going to actually dance with that guy."

"Oh, really?"

"Really," she mimicked boldly.

Large flakes of snow tumbled gently around them as they walked back to the condo. Charli ran off the shoveled pathway, frolicking like a child as her feet made designs in the freshly fallen snow.

"This stuff is like powder," she declared, bending to scoop up a handful of the fluffy flakes and toss them into the air.

"Are you going to come inside or are you going to play in the snow?" Max called out to her as he inserted his key in the lock.

The carefree, impish look disappeared from her face and he felt a stab of remorse for having stopped her fun. She followed him inside and was all business as she removed her jacket and boots, saying little to him.

"What time am I expected to be at work tomorrow?"

Max shrugged. "You can sleep in if you like. My brothers won't be arriving until after noon."

With a polite good-night, she left the room. All Max could think about was how, for the first time in his life, he had wanted to know how to country-western dance.

CHAPTER FIVE

WHEN Charli woke the following morning, it was still snowing. The flakes were no longer light and fluffy. Instead they were like tiny darts being tossed and turned by a fierce wind that created a mass of white which obstructed the view of the mountains.

Downstairs, she was greeted by the crackle and snap of logs burning in the fireplace. The first floor of the condo was actually one great room with the kitchen and dining area on one end and a massive stone fireplace and living area on the other.

Max was sitting at the kitchen table engrossed in the *Wall Street Journal*. It was the first time she had seen him in anything but a suit. Her heart took an extra beat at the sight of him in a forest green sweater and navy slacks.

His brow was wrinkled, his lips tight as he read the paper. Charli wondered if it were stock prices causing him to scowl or if he simply was grumpy at this time of day.

When she said good morning to him, the lines in his forehead deepened.

"There's coffee on the stove and muffins on the counter," he mumbled without lifting his nose from the paper.

"Thanks." Charli tried to ignore his sour mood. As she passed him she caught the aroma of the pine-scented soap she had purchased for him.

While she poured herself a cup of coffee, he pulled his laptop computer from its case and set it on the table. In moments he had hooked up the phone modem and was sending a fax.

"I thought you were on a holiday," Charli commented.

"I am," he answered absently, his fingers busy on the keyboard.

There was silence except for the popping of the logs in the fireplace and the sound of the computer's keys being stroked. Charli felt superfluous watching him work. He didn't need her there. He had his computer, the telephone and the *Wall Street Journal*.

"Is there anything you'd like me to do?" she offered.

He looked at her as though he wanted to say something, but then shook his head and returned to his work.

Charli snooped around the kitchen, opening cupboards and checking the refrigerator for its contents. Her stomach growled. A muffin may be enough for Max Taylor for breakfast, but she needed more.

"If you'd like me to make you some breakfast, I will," she felt obliged to offer.

That brought Max's head up with a jerk. "I promised you that you wouldn't have to cook this weekend. It wasn't in your job description."

"Maybe I'm not offering as a professional courtesy," she said coyly.

He smiled then. A wonderful, charming smile that showed Charli the reason why Max Taylor was the object of so many women's affection.

"Then I'll accept your offer. Two eggs over easy, bacon crisp."

For the umpteenth time Charli wished they weren't alone. She needed other people around. Anyone who would distract her from her boss's good looks.

She was about to ask him if he wanted toast with his eggs when the phone rang. Although she tried not to eavesdrop on his conversation, she couldn't help but overhear. At the mention of bad weather, she automatically glanced outside and saw that snow had drifted in front of the sliding-glass door.

"That was my brother, Gerr," Max told her as he hung up the receiver. "His flight's been delayed because of the snow. He doesn't think he'll be here before tomorrow."

"What about your other brother?"

"Larry? I don't expect he'll be here any sooner. The problem isn't on the Minnesota end. They've closed the Bozeman airport because of the storm.''

Charli felt a brief moment of panic. "You mean, we're stuck here?''

"We weren't exactly planning on going anywhere, were we?'' he asked with a chuckle.

His casual attitude annoyed her. She turned her back to him and pulled a frying pan from the cupboard. It hit the top of the stove with a thud.

"I can't believe this is happening,'' she grumbled.

"What? That you're cooking breakfast or you're in a Montana blizzard?'' Again his tone was flippant and Charli's perkiness was nowhere to be found.

She glared at him. "Both.''

"You don't need to worry about the storm. We're safe here and we've plenty of food.''

Charli wondered how safe it was to be snowbound with a man who could make her insides feel like gelatin. Despite her intention to regard him as her boss, she was beginning to feel close to him. How could she not? She had picked up his shirts from the cleaners, shopped for his personal care items and now she was cooking him breakfast.

"Real safe,'' she mumbled sarcastically.

"You're from Minnesota. A little snow shouldn't bother you.''

She didn't appreciate his attempt to be amusing. Well, she would show him just how funny he was.

Without another word she cooked breakfast—her way. Oatmeal with a sliced banana. When she set Max's share in front of him, he grimaced.

"What's this?"

"Breakfast."

"Yes," he said sarcastically, "if you're my nephew Jeremy."

Charli sat down across from him. "Your nephew's lucky he has such a smart mother."

Max glanced over his shoulder to the kitchen. "So where are the bacon and eggs?"

"In the refrigerator," she answered, then dug into the oatmeal.

"This is all you cooked?"

"Mmm-hmm. Try it. Oatmeal is the perfect food for a blizzard. It warms you up," she said in a saccharine voice. "And it doesn't have all the fat and cholesterol of those other things."

Max didn't respond. He stared at the cereal for several moments, then fixed Charli with a glare which she chose to ignore. He finally sprinkled a liberal dose of sugar on the oatmeal and began eating.

Halfway through their silent meal the phone rang again. When Max returned to the table he said to Charli, "I'm going to go to the post office."

She glanced outside. "Do you think the roads are plowed?"

"Plowed or not, I have to go."

Charli walked to the window overlooking the garage. "The main road is open, but you'll never get your car out. There are huge drifts in your way."

"I'll call and get someone over here right away." Again Max went to the phone. After several heated conversations that all ended with his slamming the receiver down on the cradle, he pulled his parka from the closet.

"Is someone coming?" Charli asked.

"The earliest anyone can get here is this evening." He tugged on a pair of boots. "By then the post office will be closed."

"You're not going to try to drive through that mess, are you?"

"I'll shovel first."

"Shovel? It'll take you all day!"

"As long as I finish before the post office closes." He slipped a hat on his head and disappeared out the door.

Charli grabbed her brand new yellow ski parka and bib pants. Within minutes she was outside wading through the knee-deep snow.

"Where are you going?" Max called out to her as she headed toward the lodge.

"To find you a plow."

"It can't be done."

"I can do it," she shouted back to him. Since she didn't turn around, she didn't see the dubious look on his face. "Max Taylor may know everything there is to know about finance," she said to herself as she trudged through the snow, "but he has a few things to learn about life and I'm just the one to give him a lesson."

Max had forgotten how heavy snow could be. He hadn't shoveled since he had been in college and he wasn't happy to be doing it now. As he paused to stretch his muscles, a pickup with a plow on front pulled up in front of his driveway.

When Charli, all bundled up in her yellow skiwear, jumped out of the cab, he could only stare in disbelief.

"Wes is going to help us out," she announced with a grin.

Wes was a big man with a beard and a cowboy hat. He waved at Max, then maneuvered his pickup back and forth, the metal plow on the front scraping and grinding as it shoved the huge drifts of snow to the side of the driveway. In less time than it had taken Max to shovel the walkway, he had cleared away all the snow.

"Wait here. I'll be right back," Charli told Wes when he had finished the job.

Max watched her disappear inside. He thanked Wes effusively and pulled out his wallet. "What do I owe you?"

Wes didn't answer the question, but asked, "So, you're on your honeymoon, are you?"

"Er...yes." Max pulled several bills from his wallet, but Wes ignored them.

"Your wife sure is something. You've got yourself a honey," the burly man said enviously. When he realized Max was shoving money at him, he waved it away. "That's not necessary."

"Charli paid you?"

Just then Charli came bouncing out of the house. "Here you go, Wes." She handed the thick-set man a round tin.

"Thank you. You folks have a Merry Christmas now," he said as he climbed back into the cab of his truck. With a toot of his horn, he drove away.

"What did you give him?"

"Rum balls. My mother makes them every year at Christmas. I brought a tin of them to share with your family, but I thought Wes should have them for being so sweet. I mean, it was awfully nice of him to come help you when he already had seven people on his waiting list."

Max stared at her in disbelief. He couldn't figure out how she had been able to talk the man into doing his driveway before the others. Certainly not by offering him a tin of rum balls?

"How much did it cost me to be at the top of his list?" he wanted to know.

"Max, why are you even asking such a question? The point is, you couldn't get anybody to do it for you. I did."

Max knew she was right. She had accomplished something he had failed to do. No wonder she was successful with her business. She was resourceful and tenacious. And still managed to look like an elf in bumblebee clothing.

"Want to go for a ride?" he asked as he held the door to his car open.

Charli didn't hesitate. "Sure."

"Good. We'll stop for lunch on the way back— since we didn't have much breakfast," he said with his tongue in cheek.

After a stroll through the ski shops of Big Sky, Max took Charli to a small restaurant that reminded her of an old Western saloon. It had a wooden floor that creaked and wagon wheel chandeliers hanging from the ceiling.

It was not the kind of place Charli expected a man like Max to enjoy. She had expected they'd dine on linen tablecloths with men in white shirts and cummerbunds who swept away their crumbs.

But then, sitting across from him watching him eat barbecued beef on a bun, she realized that he was a different person when he was in the ski resort than he was back home in the corporate world. She liked the Montana Max much better than the Minnesota Max, as dangerous a thought as it was.

When the waitress asked if they wanted any dessert, Max truly won her heart when he chose the hot-fudge ice cream delight.

"I'd love to try it, but I don't think I could eat one," Charli said, eyeing the dessert as it was delivered to a nearby customer. "Could I get half of one?" Charli asked the waitress.

The waitress shook her head and said, "I'm sorry. I can bring you an extra plate if you want to try some of his." She pointed her ink pen at Max.

Embarrassed, Charli replied, "Oh, no, that's all right."

"Bring an extra plate," Max instructed the young woman. To Charli he said, "After you gave up your rum balls for me, I can share my hot-fudge ice cream delight with you. Besides, I'm sure there is plenty for both of us."

It wasn't the thought of depriving Max of part of his dessert that made Charli nervous. It was the intimacy of sharing it with him. She felt like she was sixteen again and sharing a soda with her high school flame at the malt shop.

"This is a delight, isn't it?" she said as she savored the chocolate dessert.

"Definitely makes up for the bacon and eggs," he added, giving her a wry grin.

"You were making fun of me."

"I was not."

Her response was one raised eyebrow.

The Editor's "Thank You" Free Gifts Include:

- Four BRAND-NEW romance novels!
- A beautiful cherub magnet!

PLACE
FREE GIFT
SEAL
HERE

YES!

I have placed my Editor's "Thank You" seal in the space provided above. Please send me 4 free books and a beautiful cherub magnet. I understand I am under no obligation to purchase any books, as explained on the back and on the opposite page.

116 CIH CCQ7 (U-H-R-12/97)

Name

Address   Apt.

City

State   Zip

Thank You!

DETACH AND MAIL CARD TODAY!

Harlequin Reader Service® — Here's How It Works:

Accepting free books places you under no obligation to buy anything. You may keep the books and gift and return the shipping statement marked "cancel." If you do not cancel, about a month later we will send you 6 additional novels, and bill you just $2.67 each plus 25¢ delivery per book and applicable sales tax, if any.* That's the complete price, and—compared to cover prices of $3.25 each—quite a bargain! You may cancel at any time, but if you choose to continue, every month we'll send you 6 more books, which you may either purchase at the discount price…or return to us and cancel your subscription.
*Terms and prices subject to change without notice. Sales tax applicable in N.Y.

If offer card is missing write to: Harlequin Reader Service, 3010 Walden Ave., P.O. Box 1867, Buffalo, NY 14240-1867

BUSINESS REPLY MAIL
FIRST-CLASS MAIL   PERMIT NO. 717   BUFFALO, NY

POSTAGE WILL BE PAID BY ADDRESSEE

HARLEQUIN READER SERVICE
3010 WALDEN AVE
PO BOX 1867
BUFFALO NY 14240-9952

NO POSTAGE
NECESSARY
IF MAILED
IN THE
UNITED STATES

"Tell me. How did you get Wes to plow my drive?" he asked, leaning forward with both arms on the table so that his face was only inches from hers.

"Trade secret."

"Do you have a lot of trade secrets?"

"Enough to keep me employed," she answered coyly.

He grinned. "You do quite a good business at Almost A Wife, don't you?" There was admiration in his tone.

"People live busy lives. They appreciate having a service they can turn to for help."

Curious, he asked, "How did you come up with the idea?"

"After I graduated from college I couldn't find a job, so one of my roommates suggested I start my own business." She took another scoop of the ice cream, then said, "One thing I noticed about most of my friends who had found full-time careers was that they always seemed to be complaining about not having time for doing all those little things their mothers always did. One of my friends actually said to me she wished she could have a wife."

"And that triggered the idea for your business?"

She nodded. "I like shopping, and I enjoy organizing parties, and I had plenty of experience. You see, when I was in college I was the one in the dorm who would do ironing, laundry, and run errands—for a small fee, of course.''

''Is that how you worked your way through college?''

''Pretty much. Not everyone has a trust fund.''

''I sense a criticism in that statement.''

''There was none intended.''

''I'm glad to hear that. You see, I, too, worked my way through college. When I wasn't painting houses, I was working at a warehouse.''

She cocked her head and looked at him, prompting him to ask, ''What are you doing?''

''I'm trying to picture you in painter's overalls and a brush in your hand.''

''It wasn't the most glamorous job in the world, but it paid my college tuition.''

Charli made a sound of understanding. ''One thing I learned early in life was that solutions are there if you're willing to look for them.''

''Which is why we're here in Montana, isn't it?''

She nodded in agreement.

''And as long as we are, we should make the most of the facilities.''

''Meaning?''

''I think we should go skiing this afternoon. With all this new snow the slopes are going to be fantastic.'' He signaled for the waitress to bring him the check.

''You can go if you like. I'll wait for you at the lodge.''

"I want you to come with me."

"I told you before we left that I don't ski. I've never had the opportunity."

"Are you saying you've never been on a pair of skis in your life?" he asked in disbelief.

"No. And for your information, lots of people haven't."

"True, but you rollerblade, you play broomball, you do aerobics, you..."

"Wait a minute. How do you know I do aerobics?" she asked.

"Sometimes I hear you before I leave in the morning," he admitted. "You seem very athletic."

"Well, skiing is not in my athletic inventory."

"Maybe it's time you added it."

She didn't want to admit to him that the thought of flying down a slippery hill on two sticks was terrifying. "I'll pass."

"What happened to the Charli who says 'I can do it' to any challenge?"

He had a point. If she turned down his offer she would look like she was afraid. If there was one thing Charli never did it was back away from a challenge.

"I don't have skis." She made one last attempt at a protest.

"We'll rent you some."

"All right. I'll do it."

"Good."

The look in his eye once again had Charli wondering if she hadn't made a mistake letting her emotions rule her head. Was she really accepting his offer because it was a challenge or because the thought of spending the afternoon with Max was too tempting to resist?

Charli's courage deserted her as Max pulled her toward the ski rental building. "I think I left the water running in the bathtub."

"Let it run over."

"And I didn't turn off the teakettle. I'm sure it's boiling by now...."

"I checked the stove. It was off."

"I'm expecting a phone call...."

"Give it up, Charli. You're going to ski, like it or not." He gently nudged her toward the waiting line. "You've already made up every lame excuse and I don't accept any of them. Relax. It's going to be fun."

"How can I relax? I feel like such an amateur!" She gazed forlornly around the large room filled with rental skis, poles and boots. The equipment was so foreign to her it might as well have been from an alien planet. Whatever had made her think she was going to enjoy this? Even being this close to Max—with his arm around her to keep her from running back to the condo— wasn't worth the knot of nervousness in her stomach. She could *break* something doing this! Something she might need—like a leg.

"I'm sure the fellow in front of you hasn't had any more experience than you, Charli," Max assured her, amusement heavy in his voice.

Charli eyed the party in question. He was three years old, if that. The child had curly blond hair, a wide smile and a sparkle of excitement in his eyes as his father lifted him to the tabletop where the skis were fitted so he could see his very own miniature skis come off one of the racks.

"That child should be home with a baby-sitter," Charli groused. "What kind of parents would try to teach a three-year-old to ski?"

"Lots of them, by the look of it."

Charli glanced around. Max was right. There were several youngsters being fitted for equipment.

"In fact, one of my nephew's Christmas gifts is ski boots, and he's only two."

"Some uncle you are. He could get hurt!"

A man thrust a pair of skis and poles into Charli's hands and Max led her toward the door.

Max tipped his head toward the beginner's slope. Several young parents were skiing down the hill with tiny children on skis braced between their legs. "Now's the time to learn, when he's not afraid of falling. Kids roll like little balls of butter. It's adults that stiffen up and break their bones." He knelt down to clip Charli's boots into her skis. Having him kneeling like that at her feet gave Charli a funny, tingling feeling in her belly.

She resisted the urge to reach out and touch his hair.

"I can't do this, Max. I need all my parts intact. I can't be a good wife to you if I'm on crutches."

"Then I'll wait on you. Isn't that what good husbands do?"

The thought sent a skitter of electricity through Charli. She clenched her teeth and sucked in her tummy. All right, Max Taylor, if you're going to force me to do this, then let's get started!

Her resolve lasted all of sixty seconds. The minute she moved forward on the skis, it felt as though the earth was sliding from beneath her feet. "Max, I...."

He caught her beneath her armpits and braced her against his chest. "Slowly now, you can do it. It's only a few more feet to the platter tow."

"What's that?" Charli was not the type to be "towed" anywhere.

"There. That. We'll stand in line. When your turn comes, the girl at the front will slip that platelike disk suspended from those ropes between your legs. It will brace you at the backs of your thighs. Hang on to your poles and the rope and let it pull you to the top of the beginner's slope. Then ski off. I'll be on the next platter. Just wait for me."

Charli eyed the contraption. People were skiing up the side of the hill with apparent ease. When her turn came at the front of the line, she braced herself. The attendant caught a rope and platter and thrust it between Charli's legs. It rested at the backs of her thighs with a comforting solidness. Charli leaned back to let the tow do its work.

The next thing she knew she was flat on her back in the snow with Max looking down at her in befuddlement. "Don't rest your *full* weight on the platter, Charli. Hang on to the rope. The platter is only meant to help you keep your balance, not to drag you up the hill."

"You could have told me that earlier," she growled as Max righted her again. A child, five years old or so, glided by her and waved on his way up the hill.

It took three more attempts before Charli managed to master the tow and travel halfway up the hill. She dropped the rope, tried to ski forward and landed in a heap at Max's feet.

"You weren't kidding when you said you didn't know anything about skiing, were you?"

"I don't 'kid.' In fact, I left my sense of humor somewhere down the hill." To make her point, Charli tipped her head toward the bottom of the run. "Oh, dear...."

"What?"

"It's a long way down!"

Max chuckled. "It's a long way down the black diamond slopes, Charli. There's hardly an angle to this hill." To expedite matters, he put his arms around her, picked her up and turned her around.

"Now remember to keep your skis parallel as you go down."

"I can't, Max!" She was breathing hard from exertion—or excitement from Max's embrace.

"Sure you can. I'll ski backward in front of you. Keep your eyes on me. That's it. First one foot and then the other. Left. Right. Left...."

She only fell three times on her trip down the hill. It would have been positively humiliating if Max weren't so patient and if it didn't feel so divine every time he picked her up, dusted her off and gave her a squeeze of encouragement. There were icicles on her eyelashes and gleams of triumph in her eyes by the time they reached the bottom.

"Again?" Max wondered.

Because she didn't want to disappoint him, Charli nodded.

Repeatedly they made the trip up the slope and painstakingly traveled down. Finally Charli made it to the bottom without falling even once.

Triumphantly she skied into the level area at the bottom of the slope grinning like a cockeyed Halloween pumpkin. Max let out a whoop of appreciation and grabbed her in his arms. Before either of them knew what they were doing, they were embraced in a hot and icy kiss—warm lips and tongues, chilled cheeks and half-frozen noses and a blaze which was ignited deep in Charli's belly.

Max felt it, too. Heat—hot enough to melt more than the ice which had accumulated on their clothing—crackled between them.

She felt butterfly-light in his arms. Reluctantly he released her. Still a little stunned by the surge of magnetism between them, he allowed his arms to fall to his sides.

"This calls for a drink of celebration." His voice sounded surprisingly shaky.

While mentally regrouping, Charli nodded. A drink. Dozens of people around. No more excuses to fall into his arms. Yes, a drink was definitely in order.

CHAPTER SIX

A FIRE was crackling in the lodge fireplace when they entered. Dozens of people in pricey après-ski clothing were seated in couches and at small tables around the room. Max dropped into a chair close to the fire and Charli followed suit. A waitress appeared almost before Charli had a chance to pull off her hat.

"Champagne," Max said briskly, not waiting to hear what Charli might want. "Escargot and calamari."

Charli only stared at him. *Snails and squid*?

Max took her silence for acquiescence. "An order of each."

Charli waited for the waitress to drift off before she said, "You didn't have to order that for me. I would have been happy with a cup of hot chocolate."

"Getting up on skis for the first time calls for champagne. It seems *most* appropriate that we celebrate."

"But I don't think I eat squid."

"You will. It's wonderful here. Doesn't Almost A Wife do squid?" He sounded faintly surprised, as though he expected her to be more accustomed to the finer things in life.

"Apparently you're our most discerning customer." Charli kept her voice neutral, hesitant to betray the emotions she was experiencing. It made her uncomfortable to sit here enjoying such luxuries when she knew that her "marriage" was a sham and her relationship with Max a farce. Besides, even though Max apparently expected otherwise, she was unaccustomed to such luxuries. Dinner at a fast-food restaurant had been the way she and her mother had celebrated big occasions. Champagne and escargots were a long way from shakes and fries.

"Getting warm?" Max was eyeing the yellow ski pants zippered up the front. Charli had shed her jacket, which now rested over the back of her chair.

"Yes, but the zipper is stuck. Wet maybe."

"Here, let me help you." He was tall, masculine and intimidating in black ski pants and a black turtleneck sweater as he moved around the table to her. When he bent his head to work on the errant zipper, a lock of dark hair tumbled over his forehead.

Charli froze like a deer in the headlights of an oncoming car as his hands worked so near to her breast. The warmth and scent of his body radiated around her, enveloping her in a blissful yet alarming cocoon of sensation.

"Got it." Without asking her permission, Max moved his hands to her shoulders and rested them there, light as feathers on the straps of her bibbed pants. Slowly he drew the strap down over her shoulders and arms until the quilted fabric fell away. Charli stood there feeling exposed and mesmerized.

"Are you all right?" Max peered into her eyes. "You look rooted to the spot."

Charli dropped like a brick into the chair, mortified at the places her imagination had taken her. "Fine. Okay. Sure. I mean . . ."

She was saved by the arrival of the champagne with its cork-popping ceremony. By the time their glasses were filled, Max had forgotten her odd behavior.

Charli was relieved. She would have been hard-pressed to explain it to herself. His hands so near her breasts, his head bent low over her, his leg brushing hers. . . .

She swilled down her first glass of champagne as though it were water. In the next moment, she started to cough as a fire burned in her throat.

Max handed her a glass of water. "You haven't had a lot of experience with liquor, have you?" He sounded amused.

"Sorry about that." She felt a blush rise to her cheeks. She was a veritable dictionary of emotion today, but at least for the moment she'd lost her discomfort over the money Max was spending on her.

"Tell me about yourself, Charli." It was more of a command than a question, but Max looked genuinely interested.

"There's not much to tell."

"Then tell me about your family."

"There's not much of that, either. Just me and my mom."

"No father?"

"Not for a long time." Charli didn't relish telling Max that her mother was on her fourth marriage or that her father had abandoned them when Charli was only an infant. No matter how cheerful a twist one put on a story like that, it didn't come out sounding very upbeat. And Charli needed to feel upbeat right now—as well as strong, forceful and in control—all the qualities that seemed to vanish when she was around Max.

"We moved a lot when I was a child. Mom changed jobs often, always trying to improve our lives. She's an amazing woman, Max. Resilient. Brave. Fiesty."

"Like someone else I know?" The hard angles of his face softened as he studied her.

"Those are qualities I admire. My mother is one of my heroes and one of my closest friends."

"Now tell me about you."

"What do you want to know?"

"Why does a beautiful woman give up her social life to play 'wife' to me? Wouldn't you rather be someone's real wife?"

"I was engaged once, but it didn't work out."

Max looked curious but the bitterness in her voice kept him from enquiring further. Instead he spilled the last of the bottle of champagne into Charli's glass.

As he did so, an attractive, slender, long-legged woman sidled up to their table. She appeared to be engaged in some sort of mating dance the way she was swinging her hips and puffing her chest so that her bustline was shown to its best advantage.

"Max, is that you?" Her voice was breathless and excited.

"Marlene?"

"How are you, Max? It's been ages! And you look more wonderful than ever!" The woman spoke as if there were exclamation points behind every sentence.

"I could say the same about you." He pulled a devastating smile out of his repertoire. "I didn't know you skied."

"Black diamonds," she boasted, referring to the most difficult runs at the resort. "They are the only ones that are any fun."

Charli gave the woman a cross-eyed glare but neither she nor Max noticed. The last bit of champagne tasted bitter in her mouth. It had been sweet until she realized what a foolish, inconsequential thing she and Max had been celebrating. She'd gone down the *bunny* hill alone, for heaven's sake! And Max and Marlene were now comparing notes about ski runs that would have turned Charli's blood cold.

She took a vicious bite of calamari and savored the gummy crunch between her teeth, wishing she could snap someone's head off just as easily—preferably Max's.

That thought startled Charli to her senses. What did it matter to whom Max talked? She didn't care—or at least, *shouldn't* care. She was his employee and it was her job to remember that her position was pretense, not reality. Hirling, not wife.

Calmer now, Charli observed Max as he talked to the lovely Marlene. What had happened to the man who was utterly determined to keep predatory females away? Wasn't that the reason she was here? To provide him with the persona of *family man*? In fact, Max had forgotten her—his new bride—entirely.

With perverse enjoyment, Charli decided to remedy that fact.

"Max, honey, aren't you going to introduce me to your friend?" She put a possessive hand on his wrist, flashing the gold wedding band Max had insisted she wear.

If Max's stare had been a laser, Charli would have been history.

Stiffly he turned to her. "Marlene, I'd like you to meet my wife, Charli. Charli, this is Marlene Cramer, an old friend of mine."

"A wife? That's a new twist, Max." Marlene looked Charli over and dismissed her much as she might a fly buzzing over the empty serving plates. "Tell me what else is new."

Amazed by the nerve of the woman and the insensitivity Max was showing, Charli glowered in her chair for as long as she could without erupting. Finally, when it became obvious that Marlene didn't *care* whether Max was married or not, Charli gathered her jacket and hat and stood up.

She'd forgotten for the moment that she was still wearing her ski boots. The heavy, unbending contraptions nearly sent her sliding back into her chair, but she remained upright through sheer willpower. Max and Marlene looked up at her curiously.

"It's obvious that you two have some catching up to do. I think I'd like to take a bath and get ready for bed, so if you'll excuse me...." Wanting to annoy Marlene, she leaned over Max's dark head to kiss him. Thinking she was in control, she allowed her lips to linger a moment too long. Much to her surprise, she felt Max respond. When the kiss ended, they were both breathless.

Stunned, Charli tottered away on her boots trying to muster up every bit of dignity she could.

When she reached the door, she glanced backward over her shoulder. Max didn't look happy. Marlene had moved closer to him. He glared at Charli, who gave her head a rebellious toss and exited the room as best she could in the ridiculous boots.

Legs trembling, she hurried down a hallway.

"If he wanted to stay away from women like that one so badly, then why did he greet her with such open arms?" she muttered, startling a housemaid carrying an armload of towels. "How am I supposed to know who he wants to talk to and who he doesn't?"

And why did he kiss me like that?

She went to the front door of the lodge and stared out at the night sky. It was inky black. Puffy white snowflakes were drifting down, dancing in the floodlights outside the door. It would have been beautiful in any other circumstances.

"Need a ride somewhere, miss?" a grizzled old bellman inquired.

Within minutes she was back at the condo, tipping the driver and breathing a sigh of relief. She needed to be away from Max. He was far too troublesome to take in large doses. Deceptive, too. He could charm her socks off and then be taken in by the likes of the beautiful and glandular Marlene.

Charli wondered if she'd ever understand men—especially the ones about whom she cared. Even worse were men who treated their women like property. She'd been engaged to one of those. She'd been young and easily impressed when she'd met Griffith Parks. Both college students, Griffith was attending university because of a healthy trust fund while Charli worked thirty hours a week to pay her tuition. Griffith's easy life and cavalier attitude toward what Charli worked so hard to achieve had fascinated her. What made a man like Griffith tick? Acquisitiveness. Self-interest. A lack of consideration for the feelings, hopes and dreams of others. Sadly and too late, Charli had found she didn't like the answers.

Relief and disappointment mingled together as she entered the condo. She wanted Max to be different from the other men she'd known. Of course, if he were, then he wouldn't have needed her. He'd have a real wife and a loving relationship to depend upon.

She walked into the living room feeling inexplicably agitated. What did it matter to her who Max saw? Why should she care if beautiful women came into his life as regularly as daybreak? After all, she was only his— She caught herself as the word "wife" shimmered on the brink of her thoughts. But she wasn't his wife. Not really and not ever. She was his employee, with a six month temporary contract, and despite her rebellious body and brain, she had to remember that.

She drifted toward the kitchen to make herself a cup of coffee. On the way, she noticed that the light was flashing on the answering machine. Automatically she pushed the message button.

"Max? It's me, Gerr. We've been at the airport for five hours and they just told everybody to go home. The ticket agent says the flights in and out of Bozeman are being canceled. Looks like a no-show for us.

"Let's get together when you get back. Jeremy is terribly disappointed, but I told him you'd take him skiing in January. How's that for bribery? Must be tough to be somebody's idol. Call the house when you get in. Amy says 'Merry Christmas.'"

Charli rewound the tape and played the message again, hoping that it wasn't true. Then she hurried to the television and punched at the remote until she found the weather channel.

"That's it for tonight and tomorrow, folks. Snow and more snow. There will be no travel anywhere in the region for a couple days, so get out that book you've been meaning to read and put a log on the fire. I'll be back with satellite reports after this message."

"Oh, no!" Charli dropped into the seat across from the television. There *had* to be a way out of here. If Max's brothers weren't coming, that left her and Max alone together in this much too small and too romantic hideaway with a fireplace, a wine cellar stocked with champagne, a fridge full of groceries and a bed the size of Georgia. This was awful!

Never one to give up easily, Charli dialed the phone number of the Bozeman airport.

"Sorry, lady. No flights in or out. We aren't even going to start cleaning runways till sometime tomorrow. Nobody's flying. Keep calling, though, I imagine the storm will break pretty soon.''

Stuck. Stranded. Trapped. The idea of spending time in such close proximity to Max made Charli's body tingle. She had lost complete control of her life the day she'd met Max Taylor and now things were going from bad to worse.

But they weren't as bad as they were *going* to be, Charli realized when she heard Max's key turn in the lock. She'd flounced off in a huff at the lodge and there was no way Max was going to take that very well. That, on top of the news that his family wasn't coming, well....

Charli's fears were confirmed when she saw the look on Max's face as he strode into the room. His dark eyebrows were knit together in a fierce scowl and his lips were set like granite.

"And what was the meaning of that little scene?'' were his first words.

"I wasn't interested in your conversation, that was all. I wanted to come home and get comfortable.''

"I don't pay you to sit here by the fire. I pay you to be out in public—with me.''

"Well, excuse me. From where I sat, I appeared to be a token appendage. In fact, what I gathered from the way Marlene was looking at you and vice versa, I *was* helping you by clearing the way.''

"You play the role of a *jealous* wife very well, Charli, but that's not what I want from you. How do you think it looked?"

"Like you were having a fling without your new bride?" Charli could not stem the spill of toxic words.

"Exactly. And that could have been very costly to me." He curled and uncurled his fists as he spoke, a visible sign of his anger. "And the bottom line is this, Charli. You are hired to perform a service. You are my *employee*. No matter how offended you might be, you must remember what I've hired you to do. Is that clear?"

"Perfectly. I apologize for not being willing to stay in the same room with you while you insist on being overly friendly to a woman who is salivating over you like you're a pork chop and she's a hungry wolf. My behavior was completely inappropriate and it will never happen again."

"Before you go, you'd better finish what you started."

Charli stared at him uncomprehending until he dragged her toward him and kissed her roughly, his warm, dry lips stealing both her mouth and her heart.

Trembling and speechless, she could only stare at him.

"Don't look so surprised. You started it."

Wordless and shaking, Charli stalked into the tiny guest room next to the master bedroom and shut the door.

She woke up slowly, at first not noticing that anything was wrong. She blinked and yawned, then buried her nose a little deeper in the down comforter. It wasn't until she tried to roll over that she knew something had gone awry. She didn't move. Instead, when she kicked against the mattress, every muscle and fiber in her body screamed and refused to budge.

"What is going on here?" She tested a toe. It wiggled slightly. Her ankle was less accommodating. By the time she attempted to move her knee, she realized the extent of the muscle stiffness and pain she was experiencing.

Charli glanced in horror at the bedroom door. It looked as though it were a thousand miles away. Even getting to the edge of the bed and into an upright position seemed mind-boggling.

"Max Taylor, look at what you've done to me!" she muttered.

Gritting her teeth and giving a mighty thrust of her body, Charli managed to sit up. A fifteen-minute hot shower and an enthusiastic rub-down made her legs work again.

Still, she was glad to discover that Max wasn't up yet when she reached the kitchen. She brewed

a pot of strong black coffee and put a batch of
blueberry muffins in the oven to bake.

Movement seemed to help relieve some of the
stiffness, Charli noticed, so she continued to
work in the kitchen—frying sausage and bacon,
scrambling eggs, squeezing fresh oranges for
juice.

Much as she wanted to, it was difficult for
Charli to stay angry with anyone. It wasn't long
before she was humming as she set the table.
Perhaps a good hearty breakfast would sweeten
Max's sour mood of last night. Besides, Charli
almost admitted to herself, he was just a teensy-
weensy bit right about the way she'd behaved.
She should have stayed right there at his side—
like a good wife.

Max stood in the doorway watching her. He
was wearing a faded pair of blue jeans and
nothing more except for a bed-rumpled look and
a smile on his face.

He'd planned to stay angry with her for at least
the morning, but it was going to be impossible.
He could see that immediately. In fact, it was
going to be difficult not to laugh out loud. Charli
was moving around the kitchen like a thousand-
year-old woman, stooped at the shoulder, shuf-
fling her feet, grimacing every time she had to
raise her hand.

"A little stiff, this morning, Charli?" Max inquired with exquisite understatement.

"I have discovered muscles I didn't know I had. In fact, I don't think some of these *are* my muscles. They came from somebody buried in King Tut's tomb." She bent to remove the muffins from the oven and felt an agonizing ache in her back. "Ouch!" She shuffled away from the stove, clinging to the muffin pan. Max grabbed a pot holder from the counter, removed the teetering muffins from her grip and kicked the oven door closed with his foot.

After the muffins were safe on the counter, he steered Charli toward the couch. "Sit down."

She didn't have much choice. He gave her a light tap and she tumbled onto the couch because her muscles were too weak and cramped to hold her upright. Charli moaned.

"Pull up the leg of that thing." Max was approaching with a tube in his hand.

" 'That thing' is my Christmas outfit," Charli corrected. She had managed to pull on a pair of green leggings and a red and green sweater decorated with miniature Christmas ornaments. She looked like an elf all caught up in a Christmas tree.

Max ignored her and pushed up the fabric on one leg. Then he squirted a glob of white, toothpastelike stuff into his hand and began to massage her calf. The air was permeated with the pungent medicinal smell of liniment.

"Oh! Ow! Oh, oh . . . ahhh!"

"Better?" Max leaned back and watched the blissful expression on Charli's face as she discovered that she could move her foot again.

"Have you got enough there to do my whole body?" Charli wondered, ecstatic with relief. Then the meaning of her words sank in. "I didn't mean...I just wanted you to...I just meant...."

The atmosphere in the room had changed and it wasn't just the sharp odor of liniment. An electric charge snapped in the air that was sheer animal attraction.

Quickly, Charli covered her leg. "How about doing this later? Breakfast is getting cold." She needed some space between herself and Max.

As Max sat down to the finely set table, an appreciative expression crossed his features. "I'm impressed. You've kept up a notable tradition."

"What's that?" Charli sat down across from him, still a little edgy from his very nearness.

"Every blizzard I've ever been caught in has been associated with wonderful food. When I was younger, my brothers and I would roast marshmallows in the fire and make a sandwich of them with chocolate bars and graham crackers...."

"Smores, of course," Charli finished brightly. "I've got all the ingredients. I'd thought perhaps your little nephew might like them."

"You do think of everything, don't you?" Max's expression softened as he looked at her.

It made Charli's insides feel like they, too, were being roasted over a fire.

"I try. After all, I—Almost A Wife, I mean—aims to please."

Charli hoped Max hadn't noticed her slip. She didn't know when this job had become such a personal project, but it had. As Max's hand stole over hers, the whole thing seemed very, very personal indeed.

CHAPTER SEVEN

DID there have to be Christmas carols on *every* station? Charli wondered morosely as she twiddled with the radio dial. She was fed up with glad tidings and good cheer. It was Christmas Eve day and Charli was eight hundred miles from home. What was even more depressing was that the distance between herself and Max could be measured in light-years rather than miles. This Christmas was stacking up to be the loneliest, longest holiday Charli had ever spent.

Max was reading in front of the fire. He had only uttered about twenty words all day.

Bored and irritated, Charli clapped two pans together as she thrust them into the cupboard. Max looked up and scowled. "What is it? You've been pacing like a caged tiger."

"It's Christmas and we're stuck here! The weather. My mom...." Charli's voice grew ragged. "Oh, just forget it. You wouldn't understand."

The silence behind her stretched on for a few moments. Then Max moved toward her. Charli could feel the radiating warmth of his body against her back.

"Penny for your thoughts."

123.

"Don't waste your money." She dunked her tea bag into the now-cold cup of water beside her.

"I never waste money. It's too hard to earn. How about *two* pennies?" He slipped onto the stool beside her. "Why is it so difficult for you to be separated from your mother at Christmas?"

"I don't have much family other than my mother. Most of my life it's been me and her against the world. We lived a pretty nomadic life, I guess, but she always made Christmas special for me.

"Sometimes that meant waiting until Christmas Eve to get a tree because that was when the prices went down. Occasionally someone would take pity on us and give us one for free. We'd make decorations and drink cider and sing songs. Sometimes we'd stay up half the night watching silly old movies on our little black-and-white television set.

"Somehow, though, in the morning, Santa would have crept in and put presents under the tree. I always thought Santa was a very practical man. He gave me toothpaste, toothbrushes, deodorant, underwear, packages of pens and pencils—everything I needed throughout the year. Every little item was individually wrapped so it looked like I received a ton of gifts. And there would always be one special thing I'd always wanted but never dared even to wish for—a sweater I'd drooled over at a department store, a stuffed animal, a game—one very special thing. I don't know how my mother knew, but she always did.''

"You were very fortunate.'' There was a sadness in Max's voice that Charli couldn't identify.

"I suppose that's why I feel so lost today. Even though she's remarried, I believe she needs me as much as I need her. That's why I took this job. She's been in a financial bind.''

"What does your mother think of you working for me?''

"Mom thinks I'm crazy, pretending to be a stranger's wife for money.''

"And what do *you* think?''

"I want to get my mom out of the cycle of poverty in which she's been trapped. She's finally found a man who appreciates her. They're close to getting on their feet. With my help they can do it. You're paying me enough to do that and pay off all my loans, as well. I'd be a fool *not* to do it!''

Comprehension and surprise flickered across his features. Max's expression subtly gentled. "So you're willing to live through one Christmas without seeing your mother?''

"And you haven't been helping very much. You've sat here all afternoon pouring over papers from your briefcase.''

"It comes with the job. Besides, I'm not accustomed to having someone around twenty-four hours a day. I've had little practice at being a husband.''

''Nobody should work on Christmas Eve. It's a special holiday.''

''Maybe if you're a child, but we're adults, Charli.''

''I have an idea.'' She held out her hand to Max. ''Come on.''

''Where are we going?''

''Christmas tree shopping. Don't worry. They're cheap on Christmas Eve.''

''You think I worry about money?''

''You seemed to be obsessed about making it. I thought you wouldn't want to spend it on something as sentimental as a tree.''

''My heart isn't made completely of ice, as you might expect. Blood still pumps through at least two or three arteries,'' he said wryly.

Charli bundled into her jacket and led him to the rented car parked in the garage. They drove down the mountain into Bozeman and stopped at the first Christmas tree lot they saw.

''These trees are grown right here in Montana,'' the owner assured them. ''Fresh as fresh can be. Feel these needles—soft and supple. These trees will last a month.''

Max raised an eyebrow but didn't say anything. Charli could read his mind, however. All Max needed was a tree for a day or two. He couldn't care less about next month.

"These are beautiful," Charli said, her breath a visible vapor in the crisp winter air. She stroked the branch of a massive spruce. "This would look wonderful near the fireplace."

"Won't this do?" Max was eyeing a blue-flocked tree mounted in a tree stand. "It's ready to go."

"Blue flocking? For Christmas?" Charli nearly cried as she looked at the hideous, artificial-looking thing. "What do you plan to decorate it with...pop-top openers and tin foil balls? It's so ugly!"

"It's got a nice shape," Max said. "You'd hardly know it was blue once you decorated it."

Her shoulders sagged and she looked very much like a small child who'd just been told Santa and the Easter Bunny had had a midair collision and would be missing both holidays this year.

The salesperson picked out a white spruce. "How about this one?"

Charli's eyes brightened immediately. She clapped her mittened hands together with glee. "Oh, yes! It's perfect!"

"We'll take it." Max sighed as he put a wad of bills into the man's hand. "If you'd put it into a tree stand and tie it to the roof of the car, we'll be back to pick it up."

The gentleman grinned widely. "Yes, sir! It will be here when you return."

"What did you pay him?" Charli wondered as they headed for the Trim-the-Tree Shop.

"Enough."

Charli eyed the picked-over walls of decorations and turned up her nose. "I need red and green construction paper, ribbon, popcorn and cranberries, that's all."

"How about this?" Max held a wad of glittering tinsel in his hand.

"Oh, I suppose, but you have to promise to put it on one strand at a time. I don't like trees that looked like they've been used for tinsel target practice."

"I never realized you were such a taskmaster," Max commented.

As they drove back to the condo, snow was falling heavily again and the roads were growing less navigable with every passing hour.

Once they were home, Charli became a whirlwind of activity in the kitchen, popping corn, digging out scissors and tape and humming to herself as Max dragged the tree into the living room.

"Now what?" he wondered.

"We have to name it."

He looked as though Charli had taken complete leave of her senses.

"Name it. I name every Christmas tree."

"Why? They aren't people."

"Don't you have any Christmas spirit?"

"All right, call it Alfred." Max shrugged out of his coat and dropped it into a heap on the floor.

"Not that kind of name! The name of a famous person—a movie star or politician."

"So what do you want to call it?" Max gave the tree dubious glances as if he were wondering how the two of them—he and the tree—had gotten into such a foolish predicament.

"Just look at the tree for a while. It will start to remind you of someone. Is it tall and stately? Short and dumpy? Crooked and bent to one side?"

"I get it. The crooked one must be a politician!" Max said.

"Exactly. In my lifetime I've had trees named Richard Burton, Winston Churchill, Sylvester Stallone... I've never had an Elvis Presley. The tree is big, broad and strong-looking, don't you think? Maybe Elvis...."

"This is a classy tree. Debonair. Elegant in a rapscallion sort of way," Max offered, getting into the spirit of Charli's game. "How about—"

"Clark Gable!"

"Okay, now that's settled," Max stated.

"First we'll string popcorn and cranberries."

"Not me."

"Would you rather tie ribbons and make paper chains?"

Max scowled fiercely but Charli refused to be put off.

"Here, have some hot, spiced cider. It will put you in the mood for tying bows."

"I doubt anything could do that," Max grumbled. "When I said you could get a tree, I..."

"Hush, listen to this." Charli's eyes were shining, a sure sign that, for the moment at least, her homesickness was at bay. And tall, green and handsome Clark Gable was responsible for that. "It's my favorite Christmas song." She put a finger to her lips as the radio played "Silent Night." "Nice, isn't it?"

A short while later, Max pushed away from the table and grasped his mug of cider in one hand. "That's it. I've strung all I'm going to string."

"What are you doing?" Popcorn rained across the floor as he got to his feet.

"Every employee deserves a work break once in a while. What do you think you're running here? A sweatshop Christmas ornament factory?" He stretched out on the leather sofa in front of the fire.

The logs were at their brightest, glowing with yellow-orange flame and crackling noisily. The snow had come back full-force. The windows were nothing but blank walls of white, shutting them off from the rest of the world.

"You can't quit now—we're almost done!" Charli pleaded, hands on her hips.

"Careful, Charli. You're starting to sound like a real wife," he warned, a teasing light in his eyes.

"You think I'm nagging you?" she asked in disbelief.

"I think you're very good at getting things done." Max patted the cushion beside him on the leather love seat in front of the fire. "Why not sit for a few minutes? It's Christmas."

Automatically, Charli sat.

Their legs brushed together as the cushions shifted under their weight. The buttery leather molded itself to their bodies. Charli sank back with a delighted sigh. "Heavenly." It was only after she spoke that she realized that her head was resting neatly in the crook of Max's elbow.

She should have moved away, but her will had left her. Instead Charli pressed even further into the seat. It was Christmas Eve. Couldn't she let her guard down for just tonight?

Apparently not. Max's arm tightened around her shoulders and she realized that the emotions he was feeling had nothing whatsoever to do with Christmas. The lines of his face had hardened with intensity and desire.

As he gathered her close to him, she attempted to push away, her palms flat against his chest. "This isn't a good idea."

"Why not? What can it hurt? We're here, alone. Everyone thinks we're married. What's wrong, Charli? Aren't you the type of girl who likes to play 'house'?''

"That's the operative word, 'play.' This isn't real, Max. This is fantasy. There are some things I'll do for fantasy, but not this."

"Then how about for money? That seems to motivate you pretty well." He regretted the ill-chosen words as soon as he'd spoken them. Single-handedly he'd spoiled their romantic moment.

Charli drew a sharp breath, feeling as if she'd just been slapped. "How *dare* you, Max Taylor?" Tears stung the backs of her eyes. Is that what she was to him? A woman willing to sell her body, too?

How could a man grow to hate women so? she wondered as she scrambled away from Max as he glowered on the couch. How deeply had he been hurt to want to lash back like that? A man like Max was poison to a woman, Charli decided, a sip of hemlock all dressed up in a deceptively handsome package.

Poison. That's what he was. And she wasn't going to let herself forget it again.

She was supremely grateful for the interruption the ringing telephone provided.

"Merry Christmas, Charli," her mother said with false cheerfulness.

Hearing her voice sent a rush of homesickness flowing through Charli. "Merry Christmas, Mom. How are you and Bill getting along?"

"Everything's lovely, dear. What about you and your..." She paused to clear her throat before saying, "Boss's family? Is it a happy gathering?"

"Everything's great," Charli lied, her eyes misting over. They spoke about the usual holiday things for several minutes. Finally, she had to end the conversation or risk crying on the phone.

"We're about to eat dinner here, Mom. Wish Bill a Merry Christmas for me."

As hard as she tried, Charli couldn't prevent the tear that slid down her cheek as she hung up the receiver.

She busied herself in the kitchen, working quietly, avoiding Max's probing glances.

"You accepted this job, Charli," he finally reminded her.

"It's December 24th!"

"And tomorrow's December 25th and the day after that's the 26th of December."

She faced him with her hands on her hips. "One day is just like another and one woman is just like another. Is that what you're saying?"

Max chose to ignore the oblique reference to what had just happened between them. "Christmas is just one day out of the year."

"Not for me it isn't. It's everything that's important to me."

"You'll have to forgive me, but I've never been sentimental over holidays. If that makes me some kind of monster, then I guess I'm a monster."

"Fine. As soon as we're finished eating, you can go back to your bows," she said churlishly, putting the food on the table with more force than was necessary.

"I didn't say I wanted to work," he said as he sat down at the table.

"Oh, go ahead. I wouldn't want to make you do something silly and sentimental when you could be having all that fun with your keyboard," she drawled sarcastically. "So it's Christmas Eve. Big deal."

"Apparently it *is* a big deal to you."

"That doesn't mean you have to entertain me. I promise I won't cry myself to sleep."

They ate dinner in silence.

When they had finished, Charli insisted she clean up. After all, it was what she was paid to do, she reminded him. Max didn't argue.

As the hands of the clock moved closer to midnight, Charli could feel herself becoming more morose. Instead of enjoying Christmas, she was washing dishes for a cold, calculating man who didn't have a sentimental bone in his body.

Or so she thought until he instructed her to put on her coat and hat.

"The Taylor family may not have as many traditions as the McKennas, but we do have one or two."

"Will you be able to drive anywhere in this weather?"

"Oh, we're not going by car."

When Charli stepped outside she discovered just how they were taking this midnight adventure. Waiting at the foot of the drive was a horse-drawn sleigh.

"*This* is a Taylor tradition?" she asked as Max helped her climb up onto the black leather seat. This was a curious twist. He kept surprising her—now with this.

"We usually end up sitting on each other's laps," he answered, sliding in next to her and dragging a plaid blanket over their laps.

As the sleigh made its way across the freshly fallen snow, Charli felt as if she were taking a magical ride. The flakes had tapered off to flurries and a crescent moon hung in the sky. They could have been traveling through a video postcard everything seemed so perfect.

Bells on the horses jingled as they cruised down the quiet streets. As they rounded a bend in the road, Charli saw their destination. The lights of a small building shone like a beacon in the dark winter night.

Faint music grew stronger as they drew near. Christmas carols echoed through the night as visitors approached on foot, by horse-drawn sleighs and by skis. Instead of entering the building, everyone walked to the side where a stable had been erected, a stable that was filled not with mannequins but real people.

Max guided Charli to a spot near the front of the crowd, his arm around her protectively. There were few sounds except for the braying of a donkey as everyone slowly processed past the nativity scene. As the choir sang "It Came Upon a Midnight Clear," visitors offered their gifts to the small child asleep in the crèche. By the time Max and Charli passed the scene, there was a mountain of presents stacked at the feet of Mary and Joseph.

Max pulled an envelope from his pocket and slipped it into a basket that was overflowing with donations. As he led Charli away from the brightly lit scene, he explained the reason for the presents.

"Several local churches collect articles of clothing for families who are in need," he whispered. "This service on the mountain has become an annual tradition."

Charli reached into her pocket. "I want to give something, too."

As they entered the makeshift church, Charli saw a place for the nativity participants in front of the altar.

There was standing room only by the time everyone had come into the building. For Charli it was one of the most beautiful Christmas Eve services she had ever attended. Having Max at her side felt right and natural and her anger at him disappeared. As the layers of his complex personality fell away, she was, much to her dismay, finding herself intrigued.

Though the incident at the condo had shown otherwise, he could be kind and gentle when he chose. He was handsome. He was intellectual. As she listened to the choir singing, she mentally listed his good qualities and found the list was much longer than she had expected.

As they were exiting the church, Charli saw a gray-haired couple waving in their direction.

"Franklin! How nice to see you again," Max said, shaking the older man's hand.

"I was wondering if we were going to see the two of you with all this snow." Franklin Emmett squeezed Charli's gloved hand.

Barbara gave Charli a maternal smile that she couldn't help but respond to with warmth. When Franklin pulled Max aside, Barbara asked Charli how she was enjoying married life.

"Oh, it's been...interesting," she said, forcing a grin.

"Well, take it from someone who's been married nearly forty years. It only gets better."

"That's nice to hear," Charli responded weakly.

"You know, the minute you and Max walked into church I could tell you were newlyweds. Franklin wouldn't have had to remind me."

"Oh, really?" Charli thought she and Max must have been acting their parts well.

"It's obvious from the way Max looks at you. He couldn't keep his eyes off you." The statement was made with approval and affection.

Charli blushed, then immediately chastised herself. They were *supposed* to look like a couple in love. It was part of their business agreement. Only the problem was, she had forgotten all about their agreement and the reason she was even in church with Max.

Which meant only one thing. Without any effort on her part at all, and despite all that Max had said and done, she had fallen in love.

CHAPTER EIGHT

CHARLI did not enjoy the trip home. She was too disturbed by her discovery and too busy berating herself for falling in love with a man like Max. She had made the biggest mistake of her professional career after he had made it plain from the start that the only thing between them would be business.

Max sat as stiffly as she did, without saying a word.

Charli wondered if he was having any second thoughts about their original agreement. After all, he had kissed her and even said on one occasion that contracts could be broken. Once they were back at the condo any hope that he might regard her as anyone other than an employee was dashed.

He handed her an envelope much like the one he had left at the crèche.

"What's this?" she asked.

"It's a Christmas bonus. A token of my appreciation for a job well done," he said smoothly.

A Christmas bonus. She didn't even merit one of the gifts he had her select for his staff. Just cold, hard cash. Like the man.

139

She tried to hide her disappointment as she opened it. "You're very generous," she said coolly. "Thank you."

There was no emotion on his face as he said, "I know this wasn't an easy assignment for you."

She wanted to scream at him, "It was awful. I missed spending Christmas with my mother so I could fall in love with a man who thinks money is the answer to everything." Aloud she said, "I'm tired. I think I'll go to bed." The last few words came out on a sob. She quickly rushed from the room so he wouldn't see her cry.

Somehow she had to get through the next couple of days without revealing to Max how she felt. After all, if someone like Barbara could see that love was written all over her face, how long would it be before Max saw the same thing?

Max didn't get much sleep that night. Twice since they had been in Big Sky, Charli had cried and both times he had been responsible for her tears. He almost lost control earlier and he was paying the price for it now. He should never have asked her to sacrifice her holiday so that he could carry on a game of pretense.

He had thought that by giving her the money she claimed she needed for her mother, he could at least bring a smile to her face and make her Christmas a little less melancholy. Maybe he was wrong about her. Perhaps she wasn't as sentimental as she claimed. Could it be money was all she was really after from him?

He rubbed his hand across his cheek. What was he thinking? Charli was as genuine as they came. She was unhappy. Period. She had no ulterior motives. She simply wanted to be home for Christmas.

He looked out the window. The snow had stopped. If there was any way possible, he'd get them out of Montana and back in Minnesota before the page with December 25th written on it was torn away. He'd give her the Christmas she wanted.

Before the sun had even risen, he had made the arrangements. He had found someone who could get them to Billings, where they could catch a flight home. They could be back in time for dinner.

When there was no answer to his knock on Charli's door, Max entered her room. She was curled up in a corner of the bed. She reminded him of an elf, and the twinkle that was normally in her eyes was in the slight curve of her parted lips.

Her left hand was curled up in a fist next to her cheek. He noticed the wedding band was not on her finger. He imagined what it would be like if they were really married. He could crawl into bed beside her and hold her close.

He mentally shook himself. What was he thinking? Just because Emmett had gone on and on about how right he and Charli were for each other didn't mean that it could actually work between the two of them.

Now he was in a genuine predicament. Emmett's enthusiasm over his marriage made him feel like a first-class heel. "Oh, what a tangled web we weave," he said out loud. His voice caused Charli to stir. "What have I done, Charli?"

Startled to find him in her room, she bolted upright, pulling the sheet up close to her chin. "What are you doing in here?"

"You need to get up," he said, hating the look of mistrust in her eyes. "We're leaving."

"Leaving for where?"

"Home."

"I thought there weren't any flights?"

"I've managed to find a way. You have one hour to get ready."

"But I haven't packed."

"It's either one hour or wait until tomorrow. And I really would like to be home before the Tokyo market opens."

"You're going to do business on Christmas Day?"

"You should be pleased. It's going to get you what you want—to be home with your mother for Christmas dinner."

"But . . ."

He left her looking bewildered and vulnerable. He had to leave at that moment or risk touching her, which was something he had promised during the wee hours of the morning he would not do again. Not unless they were out in public.

As he packed his things he could hear the shower running and his imagination went wild. He quickly slammed his clothes in the leather bag and snapped it shut, then went downstairs.

That's where Charli found him. He was on the phone making arrangements with the caretaker.

She stared at the tree wistfully. "We're not just going to leave Clark Gable, are we?"

"We can't take him with us."

"But he'll dry up."

"The caretaker will look after him."

"You mean, burn him, don't you?"

"Charli, you can't keep a cut tree forever."

"I know, but we've only had him up for one day." She knew she sounded like a small child, but she couldn't help herself. It was a waste of a beautiful tree. Plus, it symbolized something she had shared with Max, something she didn't want to lose.

Max changed the subject, telling her the discussion was concluded. "Are your suitcases ready?"

She nodded, still unable to take her eyes from the popcorn and ribbon-laden tree. "I don't suppose you brought a camera?" she asked quietly.

"You want to take a picture of the tree?"

She stiffened her spine. "I do every year. Some people believe in doing sentimental things like taking pictures to remind them of holidays."

He sighed, then left the room. When he returned, he was carrying a 35 mm automatic focus. "Stand in front of Clark and I'll get a picture."

As soon as the photo was snapped, Max was all business. "We'd better get moving or we'll miss our connection."

"Do you want me to take a picture of you and Clark for your scrapbook?" she asked sarcastically.

His only response was a grunt as he hoisted his suitcase and headed for the garage.

Max barely spoke a word to Charli on the way home. He was too engrossed in his laptop computer to say anything but an occasional, "Is everything all right?"

When they boarded the jet that would take them home, the flight attendant was an old friend of Max's. It was obvious to Charli that the flirtatious woman would have liked to have been more, but the wedding band on Charli's finger sparkled brightly.

"Do you have women all over the world?" she couldn't help but ask as soon as the flight attendant had moved away.

"Erika is not one of my women," he snapped.

"If you say so," she said with a lift of her eyebrows that indicated she didn't believe him for one minute.

As hard as she tried, Charli couldn't ignore the tall, statuesque blonde who continued to flirt with Max throughout the flight. She was everything Charli had always wanted to be—confident and chic. It drove Charli crazy to think of them together. Erika would not have rebuffed Max yesterday.

When the plane landed in Minneapolis, Max suggested they take separate taxis since Charli wanted to visit her mother and he would be going to the office. She couldn't help but wonder if he really was going to work or if Erika had invited him to spend the evening with her.

Her suspicions escalated when he said, "If you'd like to stay overnight at your mother's, it's fine with me."

"I'll let you know," she said cautiously as she climbed into the taxi.

He nodded and closed the door. Before the taxi had pulled away from the curb, he disappeared into the terminal.

What had she expected? That he'd stand at the curb and blow her a kiss? She shook her head. Only a fool in love could harbor such notions.

Charli tried not to fantasize what it would be like if Max and she were truly husband and wife. It was a fantasy she quickly squelched. She knew how unsuitable she was for a man like Max

Taylor. She was good at doing all the mundane chores in his life, but he needed someone with blue blood, not common, everyday red who was burdened with a vagbond past. She was nowhere nearly sophisticated enough for his social circles.

There was just one thing to do. Soon she would get a lawyer to look at her contract to see if she could get out of their agreement.

Thoughts of what Max could be doing with his old friend Erika had Charli tossing and turning on her mother's couch that night. That's why she decided not to return to the Taylor house for a few days. She needed to clear her head before she resumed her role as a pretend wife.

Unable to reach Max, she had left a message for him on his answering service and gone into the office to help Nita with the New Year's Eve rush. She was at her desk sorting through catering menus when Walker Calhoun arrived.

"Walker! This is a surprise," she said, getting up from her chair.

"Happy New Year," he said with a grin.

She returned his smile. "Happy New Year to you. Come. Sit down and tell me what brings you here."

"I want a wife," he said. "Max is a new man since he found you. I think I could use a part-time wife myself. Since you're sitting at that desk, does that mean I can have you?"

She shook her head. "Sorry. I'm tied up for at least another five months or so. But I can get

Nita to help you. Max has more than enough work to keep me occupied. Nita makes a pretty good wife, too. Honestly.'' She raised her hand as if taking an oath.

''Okay. Point me in the right direction and I'll put in my order.''

Charli pulled open a desk drawer. ''Here. You might as well fill this out first and then I'll turn you over to Nita.'' She handed him a questionnaire and a pen.

While Walker answered the questions on the form, Charli conferred with Nita.

By the time she returned to her office, Walker had finished his end of the application and gave it to Charli. ''Okay. What's next?''

Charli ran through her usual sales pitch, then explained the fee schedule. She laughed as Walker told an anecdote regarding his unsuccessful attempts at doing his own laundry. That's how Max found them—laughing together.

''What are *you* doing here?'' he asked Walker.

''Getting me a wife,'' Walker answered with a boyish grin and a glance in Charli's direction.

The hairs prickled on the back of Charli's neck at the look on Max's face. She quickly ushered Walker out the door.

''You can't work for Walker,'' Max told her when they were alone.

''This is my office, in case you've forgotten,'' she reminded him. ''And I think I'm perfectly capable of deciding whom I do and whom I do not work for.''

"I have a piece of paper that says you work for me. At my house. Or have you forgotten that?'' he asked through tightly clenched lips.

"You told me I could still run my business,'' she answered pointedly.

"Provided it didn't interfere with mine. Walker and I have mutual friends who believe you're my wife, not my employee.''

"I'm not going to be handling Walker's case. Nita is.'' She straightened the papers on her desk so she wouldn't have to notice how handsome he looked in his three-piece suit. "Why are you here?''

"I think the question should be why are *you* here? I gave you a few days off to be with your mother, not to work for other men.''

Charli didn't understand why he was so angry with her for wanting to have other clients. "Is there something in particular you want me to do?''

"Yes. I want to invite Emmett and his wife Barbara to dinner.''

Charli's skin prickled. She would have preferred not to get to know Emmett and Barbara any better. They seemed like such a nice old couple—they were people she didn't want to deceive.

"You didn't have to come all the way over here. You could have called with the details," she told him in a businesslike tone.

"I wanted to see you."

Charli's heart thumped. "Why?"

"Fishing for a compliment, Charli?"

She blushed. "Why don't you tell me the details for the party?" she said, reaching for a pencil and paper.

"I will." He took the pencil from her fingers. "Over dinner. Come."

"I'm not dressed for dining out," she told him, glancing down at her jeans.

"We'll stop by the house so you can change." His attitude allowed no protest.

Could it be that dinner was a business meeting that merited her presence or did he really want to be with her? She soon learned the answer when he took her to a French café where they sat in a booth that was separated from the rest of the restaurant by a heavy velvet curtain.

Throughout dinner Max flirted, teased and acted as if he were genuinely interested in her as a woman. All of it made Charli rather nervous.

After dinner he asked if she needed to retrieve anything from her mother's before they went home. It was almost as if they were actually married.

This feeling persisted when they returned to the house. Sitting in his kitchen discussing his schedule for the remainder of the week, Charli realized how familiar she was with his personal life.

Long after they had said good-night, she found herself having trouble falling asleep. She pulled on her robe and padded down the stairs to find him sitting in the kitchen, a pensive look on his face. All he wore was a pair of pajama bottoms.

She would have stolen away if he had not seen her.

"I—I need to get something to drink," she said, trying to avoid looking at his bare chest.

He lifted a tumbler. "You can join me for a nightcap."

Charli poured herself a glass of milk. He looked very attractive, sitting there at the kitchen table with his chest bare. So attractive, she thought it would be wise to leave.

As she moved for the door, his chair scraped against the floor. "Where are you going?" he asked.

"I-it's late," she murmured.

He reached for her wrist and closed his fingers around it.

"This is much harder than I thought," he murmured.

"What is?"

"Pretending to be husband and wife...or maybe I should say, pretending that we're not more than business associates."

"We aren't," she whispered.

"Aren't we?" He pulled her into his arms and held her so close she could feel his breath warm against her face. "Then why do I have such a difficult time resisting the urge to do this?" He kissed her mouth. "And this." His lips blazed a trail of kisses across her neck.

Charli could feel herself melting into his embrace, her body sending him the message to continue. It felt so good to be in his arms, to have him want her as much as she wanted him.

Only Max apparently didn't want her, for he pushed her away from him. "It's late—we'd better get to bed," he said abruptly, then quickly stood and left.

CHAPTER NINE

THE following morning Max appeared at her door, unshaven and bed-rumpled and gloriously sexy. "Charli, we need to talk." He settled himself at the foot of her bed.

Charli wished she'd worn her footed pajamas instead of the oversize T-shirt that barely covered her naked limbs. She tucked the blankets firmly around her legs.

"It might be more comfortable if you'd let me get dressed first." Though she chastised him, in truth, she enjoyed seeing him this way. For a moment it allowed her to pretend their "marriage" was real and not a sham.

"In the short time we've been working together we've gotten to know each other quite well, haven't we?" he commented.

The memory of last night flashed in Charli's mind and her uneasiness grew.

"You know much more about me than many of my closest friends do," he continued. "You know the size of my clothes, the brand of my toothpaste and the name of my barber."

"Wives—even pretend ones—are supposed to know their husbands better than anyone else," she reminded him.

He reached for her hand. "You have a remarkable talent for anticipating my every need." His thumb made tiny circles across her skin, sending waves of sensation through her.

"I'm just doing my job," she said weakly, trying to ignore the feelings that went skittering through her. "It's what we agreed I'd do." She pulled her hand free from his.

"True, but as my professional responsibilities multiply, so do my social obligations. Since you've been taking care of the social aspects for me, I've come to realize that I need someone to do all those wifely things for me on a permanent basis. A man in my position should have a woman at his side. Someone he can trust. That's why I've decided to marry."

The announcement came as a shock to Charli. The thought of Max married to someone else was a painful one. She wondered which beautiful woman he would choose.

"I need a wife—and not just a pretend one." He stated the fact as unemotionally as if he were quoting the stock market. "After living with me for the past few weeks, I think you can see that, can't you?"

She nodded.

"I want you, Charli. Will you marry me?"

She stared at him in disbelief.

"It would solve a lot of problems for both of us," he went on. "You wouldn't have to worry about money and I would have someone to run my home. You could still operate Almost A Wife. You might even want to expand and hire more employees. It's obvious you have more business than you can handle.''

Charli remained silent as Max continued. ''Wouldn't you like to put an end to the pretense of being husband and wife? I think I speak for both of us when I say this charade is making us uncomfortable. Don't I?''

''Yes.'' She finally found her voice. ''But two people don't get married simply because it'd be a convenient solution to a problem.''

''Maybe marriages would last longer if they did,'' Max remarked cynically. ''We understand each other, which is more than can be said for many married couples. We're approaching this from a professional viewpoint. It can be a win-win situation if you want it to be.''

Charli could only gaze at him in disbelief. He was talking about marriage as if it were a business merger.

''But what about love?'' she blurted.

''There's something between us, Charli.''

She blushed.

''Maybe it's not love, but I don't think we'll have a problem sharing a hotel room. Don't look so shocked. It's a little awkward to travel with one's wife and ask for separate rooms.''

Again her face warmed. He wanted their relationship to be legitimate in every sense of the word. They might be marrying for convenience sake, but he would exercise his marital rights.

She wondered what he would say if she told him she was in love with him. Would he withdraw his proposition? She was convinced that's all it really was—a business proposition, not a true marriage proposal.

"You don't have to give me an answer today," he told her when she remained pensive.

"I couldn't."

His gaze met hers. For an instant Charli thought she could almost see a reflection of herself cowering beneath the bed covers in the dark recesses of his eyes.

"If we did marry...and I say that hypothetically...and we shared a hotel room, would it be one bed or two?" She wanted to know.

"One, Charli. I'm human, you know."

Her stomach felt as though she'd just ridden a rollercoaster from its highest peak to inches from the ground. She wished he was as willing to share his heart as he was his bed.

"What about other women?" she asked. Max's phone had quit ringing since the announcement of their "marriage," but occasionally Charli would still hear a hang-up on the answering machine. That had begun as soon as she'd put her own voice on the tape. She knew there were women who didn't care if Max was married or not, but the sound of a wifely voice on the other end of the line discouraged some of them. What about the ones who were more persistent?

"There will be no other women in my life, Charli."

"You say that now, but what happens if you meet someone..."

Max moved up the bed until their hips touched. She felt the warm, hard muscle of his thigh against her. She wriggled to get away but only made matters worse.

If he'd noticed the electricity passing between them, he didn't let on. His face was passive, his eyes remote. "I would never humiliate you that way, Charli. You have my promise on that. I give you my word that no one will ever know that our marriage is anything but genuine."

"But what about Nita, Walker, and our families? They know about our pretense."

"That's easy. We'll tell them we fell in love. It could happen. After all, we've been alone together under my roof for some time now. It makes sense."

His answer gave her little comfort. Max could be discreet, all right. What if at some point he decided to be "discreet" with another woman? Charli knew she couldn't take it. She loved him too much, even if he didn't return that love to her.

Her emotions were already in the way of her good judgment and Max wasn't helping one bit by kneading gently at the soft, tickly spot at the inside of her knee. Then he leaned forward and took her face in his hands and kissed her. Not hard, passionate kisses, but gentle, affectionate, warm kisses that made her mind melt right along with her body. He smelled of lingering soap and dusky sleep.

Charli's senses were galvanized into action. Her limbs melted back across the bed, her lips parted, her mind drifted into the gauzy netherworld of dreams. She could feel his bare chest brush her breasts and cursed them for standing so rapidly to attention. He pressed against her as his tongue played at the corners of her lips. "Oh, Max...."

His hands somehow found the tail of her shirt and pushed it upward. As Charli realized what he was doing, her common sense finally came back to her. "Wait!"

Max's hands stilled and lay protectively across her bare back. He was breathing heavily, his eyes thick-lidded with passion. "We can make this work. Everything else is *already* working, and sex... well, I think that's going to work the best of all."

She put her palms on his forearms and guided his hands from beneath her shirt. "I've got to think, Max, and I can't if we do...this...now. You've got to give me some time."

She couldn't believe what she was saying even as the words formed on her lips. She was trapped in a ridiculous charade and in love with a man who had no intention of loving her. Why was she considering allowing herself to be even more deeply entangled in this dreadful spider's web they'd weaved?

Because she loved him.

No matter what decision Charli made now, she would be hurt. She was torn between wanting to be with Max and her fear of being used and hurt. Were a few months or even years as Mrs. Max Taylor worth the risk?

Charli's head answered the question one way, her heart, another.

It was late when Charli made her way downstairs. She hadn't slept well since last week when Max had proposed. Last night was no exception.

She expected him to be gone, but to her surprise she found him sitting at the kitchen table with a cup of coffee and the morning newspaper. The fact that he was dressed in a suit and she was in a robe made her uneasy.

She tugged the lapels of her robe closer together. "I thought you would have left by now."

"I wanted to talk to you."

The way he was eyeing her she could only guess at what her hair must have looked like. She wished she'd run a comb through it before rushing downstairs.

"You could have written a note. I would have called you."

He folded his newspaper and set it aside.

"Some things are better discussed in person. Have a chair."

Reluctantly, she sat down across from him. "What is it?"

"I need an answer from you," he said. "I have several social events coming up, some of them out of town. Dora wants to make hotel reservations and airplane tickets. If we aren't going to marry, we'll need to stay in separate rooms."

"Oh, Max, you just turn my head with all this romantic talk," Charli murmured sarcastically. He controlled his emotions like he controlled everything else around him—with an iron fist.

"I know this pragmatic approach to matrimony is distasteful to you, but we haven't much time. Besides, Charli, we're a good match. We work well together. We compliment each other in social settings. We're a *team*. Why not make it legal?"

"This isn't a simple decision to make."

"I know it isn't. But I also know it can work. Marriages are arranged all the time. We're arranging our own, that's all." He leaned forward, his eyes plundering Charli's face with their intensity. "I've worked out a prenuptial agreement to protect you, to protect me. Everything is laid out in black and white. You can take it to an attorney and have it evaluated. If there is anything in there which does not treat you fairly, we'll have it changed."

"And how long will this marriage last, anyway?" she asked sharply, hurt by his pragmatic approach.

Max grimaced and tilted his head backward. "We reevaluate the situation after one year and then again every six months unless we decide to remain married permanently."

"That's a possibility?"

"There's no harm in being an optimist, is there?"

It gave Charli some small comfort that he hadn't indicated that he wanted a definite ending to this marriage. Charli had lived her life on hope. Now she grabbed on to the only scrap of it she could find. "This all happened too fast."

Why didn't she just say "no"? Put an end to this charade. Be done with it. And done with Max....

"I need an answer, Charli. The sooner we can end the pretense, the better it will be."

"And if I don't agree to make it legal?"

"I'm hoping that isn't going to be the case," he told her in a seductive tone. He came around to her side of the table and placed a kiss on her mouth. "I want you, Charli."

She wanted to believe it would work. If he had said he loved her she would have no doubts.

Still, the last time she'd considered marriage it had been for love—and that had failed miserably. Perhaps, for her, a marriage made at the bargaining table was the only kind that *could* be successful. Would it break her heart to share her life with a man who didn't love her? Could she trust him not to hurt her?

"I'll give you one more day to think about it, Charli," he told her, then walked out the door.

She sighed. Why was everything always so difficult? What she wanted from Max Taylor was his love. She'd scrambled and scrapped for everything that had ever come to her. Even if she did throw herself body and soul into this union, would he ever view her as more than a glorified employee?

CHAPTER TEN

CHARLI was browsing through a catalog when Walker Calhoun sauntered through the door of Almost A Wife.

"Here she is, the ultimate housewife!" He dropped into the chair across from her and leaned back casually.

"Did you want something, Walker, or did you just come by to harass me?"

"Get out on the wrong side of the marriage bed today?"

"Not funny, Mr. Calhoun." Charli felt herself blushing.

"How's your...arrangement...working out?" he asked. "Good, I hope."

"Business is good, yes."

"Don't play coy with me, Charli. You know what I mean. Are you and Max getting along? Is playing house more...stimulating than you and Max had expected?"

Charli felt herself blush and cursed the way her emotions always spelled themselves out on her face.

"I can't talk about it, Walker. It's unprofessional to—"

"Oh, don't give me that, Charli! It's you and Max we're discussing! I've been watching him the past few days, wondering how things are going, but he wouldn't reveal anything as personal as his shoe size in public. I consider myself a friend to you both, and frankly, I'm concerned."

Charli's throat tightened. "Why?"

"He's acting *too* closed-mouthed. Max doesn't share his thoughts and feelings with many people, but he's always shared them with me—until now. Are you responsible for that?"

"You think he's confiding in *me* instead?" She didn't know whether to laugh or cry. "Hardly."

"How about *you*, then? Who are you confiding in these days?" Walker looked slightly rumpled and approachable as he sat there staring at her.

A tear leaked from the corner of Charli's eye. "Oh, Walker, don't be nice to me. I know how to react to cold indifference. Why don't you treat me like everyone else does?"

"By 'everyone,' I assume you mean our friend Max? Has that big lug done something to hurt you?" Walker looked genuinely alarmed.

"Oh, no. Max is a perfect gentleman. If there's a weak link in this chain, it's me."

"What do you mean by that?" Walker leaned across the desk and took her hands into his own.

"I've done a really stupid thing, Walker. Supremely stupid. I've fallen in love with him."

Walker was obviously not surprised by Charli's revelation. "Hey, worse things have happened. Max is a great guy. I think he cares about you, too."

"You're just saying that to make me feel better and you know it, Walker Calhoun. Be honest."

Walker had the grace to drop his gaze to his hands. "All right, so he's as closed-mouthed as a clam. Max is always that way with the big things in his life. Maybe it's a *good* sign. Since he hasn't said anything about you, that could mean..."

"You're really stretching it now. Give it up, Walker. Max hasn't talked about me because he doesn't care about me. I'm an employee like Dora or one of the engineers with his company, nothing more."

"You don't *understand* him like I do."

"So help me to understand. I'd love to have an idea what makes that man tick."

"Don't be hurt if Max doesn't confide in you, Charli. He never confides in women. The women in his life are the ones who have hurt him most."

"What do you mean?"

"Max's childhood was far from idyllic. In fact, it was downright miserable. His father remarried, giving Max a stereotypical wicked stepmother. She didn't want Max or his little brothers interfering in her life, and made sure they knew it. I was at their home enough to see how hard Max tried to please that woman—and how often she belittled his 'pathetic' efforts. Never—not even once—was Max able to do anything to his stepmother's satisfaction."

"How awful!" Charli cried sympathetically.

"The irony of that is that he was a brilliant child. If Max couldn't please her, no one could.

When he was ten, he worked a double shift delivering papers just so he could buy Christmas presents for his family. When his stepmother saw the gifts he had bought, she laughed.

"What's more," Walker continued, "she managed to destroy the relationship between Max and his father, as well. It's no wonder Max is bitter and cynical about marriage. Any marriage he's seen up close and personal has been a nightmare."

"I never realized..."

"How could you? Max refuses to talk about that part of his life. It's what has made him a driven man. He made his mind up long ago that he would succeed at any cost. I think he's still trying to show his stepmother that he's not as worthless as she'd claimed."

"And he *has* succeeded."

"But what about the cost? There's never been a woman in his life that he could trust. Even if there were such a woman, Max would never know. He won't let them get that close—until you."

"Right. I'm really close to him. As close as my weekly paycheck."

"Don't underestimate that paycheck, Charli. That—and this scheme of his to make you his wife—is more than he's ever offered another woman. If you ask me, there's more to this than it seems."

"Oh?" Charli kept her voice steady and hoped her face wouldn't betray her emotions. She didn't want Walker to see how much his answer meant to her.

"He's reaching out to you, testing you."

"How many times do I have to prove that Almost A Wife is a— "

"Not the business, Charli! *You*!"

She stared at him, her jaw lax. Finally she gathered her wits about her. "That's the most ridiculous suggestion I've ever heard!"

Walker shook his head somberly. "Not so. I know Max. He cares about you, Charli."

"You're wrong. I know you are. I'm a business deal, nothing more."

Walker eyed her speculatively. "Are you willing to take the chance to find out for sure?"

"What do you mean?"

"Marry him. If this is purely business, you'll know it soon enough. You can be out of it in six months. But I don't think that's going to happen."

"You're being absurd," Charli snapped.

She rapped the tip of her pen against her desk blotter. "And I see that Nita is off the phone. She can see you now."

Walker shrugged eloquently and stood up. "I'm right, Charli. I know I am."

After he left, Charli found herself staring at a stack of unpaid bills. His words echoed through her mind. Was he right? Did Max care for her even just a little? Frustrated, Charli scraped her fingers through her hair. She had so many ques-

tions and so few answers. Could she make Max
love her now that she understood his past?

Of one thing she was certain. She wanted to
try.

Max and Charli were married by a justice of the
peace in a quiet ceremony with only their im-
mediate families present. Charli wore a red suit
that Max said made her look like a firecracker.
He wasn't far off, Charli had thought, when he
made the comment with shining eyes. She did feel
like she might explode at any moment.

To the rest of the world, they appeared to be
like any other bride and groom. Charli had decided not to tell her mother why Max had proposed. If Walker were right—and Charli was
beginning to believe instinctively that he was—
they *would* be like any other newlyweds—deeply
and passionately in love.

Max had not disappointed her. Everything
about her wedding day had been perfect—the
flowers, the reception, the champagne toasts, the
spectacular kisses—and now, the traditional walk
across the threshold.

"Max, what are you doing?" she cried as he
swept her up into his arms.

"Following tradition." He kicked the door
shut, a devilish grin on his face. He carried her
up the stairs as if she were as light as a feather.

First one red high heel fell, then the other.
"My shoes!"

"They're not the only thing you're going to lose if you keep wiggling like this," he warned.

"Where are you taking me?"

"To a place I've wanted to take you for the past couple of months." His voice was low and seductive.

Charli's heart leapt into her throat. "My room's in the opposite direction," she protested weakly.

"Not anymore, Mrs. Taylor," he murmured close to her ear.

"You mean..." Her eyes finished the question.

His answer was a long, lingering kiss that had Charli clinging to his broad shoulders. "You're my wife, Charli. No more pretense."

The last thing Charli expected on her wedding night was bliss. Nor did she expect Max to announce that they were going away on a honeymoon. Four days in the warm Caribbean sunshine chased away some of her reservations about the marriage.

Moonlight strolls on sandy beaches and sun-filled days wading in the surf made Charli shove the doubts to the back of her mind. Max was a different man in the island sun and she wished the idyllic moments didn't have to end. All too soon, however, they were back in Minneapolis.

"Is that all the luggage?" Max let two shopping bags drop to the floor.

"Should be. Did you have the cabdriver check the trunk?"

"I'm going out again. He's taking me to the office."

"Oh?" Charli struggled to keep the disappointment from her features. "Already?" She had hoped Max would stay home with her tonight. Call her foolish and sentimental, but it didn't seem right that on the first night back from their honeymoon, she should be alone.

"I need to go through my mail. I'll be home as soon as I can. Don't bother with supper. I'll pick up a sandwich in one of the machines in the coffee room."

"But I..."

Max had already disappeared through the door. Charli could see him digging into his pocket for money to pay the driver. The car door slammed and Max disappeared into the oncoming dusk.

"And that's that," Charli murmured in complaint. "Wedded, bedded and abandoned. All in five short days."

She wandered through the dark, empty rooms of the house. Funny, she thought, but if Max were here, these rooms would not feel cold or empty at all. Already he'd come to mean so much to her.

She loved him. It was a love that had grown each day and each romantic night they were in the Caribbean. Together they had made magic. Away from telephones and fax machines, from clients and critics, Max Taylor was a different man. Tender, attentive, loving. All the things she'd dreamed Max could be—and all the things she'd never expected to experience with him.

She stared at herself in a mirror, remembering the first time she'd come to this house. From the first moment she'd met Max Taylor, she'd known there was something very unique and compelling about him. As his wife, she had proof positive that it was so. She had fallen deeply, intemperately and madly in love. Now, after those glorious days in the Caribbean, she no longer doubted that Max returned the emotion.

Charli changed into a pair of jeans and headed for the kitchen. Her mother had always said that the way to a man's heart was through his stomach and Charli meant to leave no avenues untouched. As she sifted flour for a cake she sang to the oldies station on the radio and danced on the tile.

She wouldn't have heard the ringing doorbell if not for a break in the music for the weather report.

Charli swung open the oversize front door to find Franklin Emmett on the other side. Emmett looked as wizened and gleeful as ever, a foxy old troll of a man with a mind and a business sense *extraordinaire*.

Charli wiped her hands on her Kiss The Cook apron. "Franklin, what a surprise! What are you doing in this part of town?"

"I'm on my way to the airport."

"Aren't you going in the wrong direction?"

"I have a meeting to attend in New York, but I wanted to drop this off on the way." Emmett bent down and picked up a lavishly wrapped box by his feet, which Charli hadn't noticed until that moment. "I'm sorry this wedding gift is so belated, but I wanted to give it to you myself, along with my congratulations on your marriage to Max."

"What a lovely gesture, but it wasn't necessary...."

She lifted the lid from the box and discovered a beautiful crystal vase inside. She was tearing open the attached note when Emmett's statement made her look up, startled.

"Of course it was. I've followed Max's career ever since he was a young pup, and frankly, I think you're one of his best career moves yet, young lady."

"Career ... moves?" Charli stammered.

Emmett waved a gnarled hand in the air. "Don't pay any attention to the way I phrase things, my dear. My wife says I sound mercenary and callous when I speak, but I'm not that way at all. What I mean is, Max has achieved every possible success in his business life, sometimes, I believe, at a cost to his *personal* life. Now he's found you and I know that you'll bring a vital balance to his life. I'm just thankful he finally woke up to how important family values can be to a thriving organization such as ours."

Career move? Balance? Family values? What on earth was Emmett talking about? He made

Charli feel more like a corporate raider's acquisition than a wife.

Suddenly Charli experienced a cold, sick feeling in the pit of her stomach. Maybe that's what she really *was*—a useful business acquisition.

"It's been years since the first time I told Max to settle down," Emmett was saying, oblivious to Charli's rocketing emotions. "At the time, I knew he was amused by my theory that men with families made better board members for my company. He said that a wife didn't make a man think more clearly—only less so. He was a very emphatic misogynist for a man his age, I remember. Of course, I didn't take offense. Max was young at the time and determinedly single. Still, he's known for a long time how I felt." Emmett was being excessively chatty and Charli knew that somewhere in this conversation there was something for her to learn.

"How you've felt?" she echoed, desperate to make some sense of what Emmett was saying.

"About the importance of having *married* men and women on my company's corporate board? Don't get me wrong, I've got single people, too, but it's the perspective of the family man and woman that really counts these days. Even politicians are embracing and espousing family values. That's what's going to get us through the tough times ahead—strong family units which support each other, the place where children can learn right from wrong, where they can experience unconditional love.'' It was apparent that Emmett felt passionately about what he was saying.

His next words hit Charli with a physical force.

''That's exactly what I told Max when I invited him to join the board of FutureTec. Not only did Max get a beautiful, talented wife, Charli, your marriage secured him a position on my board. Frankly, if you don't mind my bragging a little, it's one of the most prestigious spots in the country right now. We're making decisions that could ultimately change the face of the industry.''

Her throat felt as though it were closing. She was shaking. Emmett's words bombarded her like bullets.

''Max, brilliant as he is, simply didn't have the profile I wanted for my board. Besides, it doesn't look good to have what others may consider 'playboys' on a board as significant as this one. You've taken him out of that category, Charli, and made him eminently eligible for one of the most powerful boards in the country.'' Emmett chuckled. ''And I'll bet when you two fell in love you weren't thinking business!'' He slapped his hand to his knee, delighted with the joke he thought he'd made.

As he did so, Charli felt her life crashing down around her. It was as clear as if it were yesterday—Max staring down at her with hooded eyes, saying that he wanted her, that he needed her, but never that he *loved* her.

Then another flashback—the casual, off-handed remark he'd made to her once, something that had sounded cold and calculating but unimportant to her until now. "I'd do *anything* to be on Emmett's board, Charli. Anyone who wants to wield influence in the business arena could do it from there."

He'd do *anything*. Even commit to a step beyond their pretend marriage and to make it a real one. To tie himself to a woman he didn't love in order to grab the gold ring a position on Emmett's board offered him. To live a complete lie with no plans to ever tell the truth. To use her even more thoroughly than she'd imagined.

Disappointment and shame tasted bitter on her lips. She managed a wooden smile and weak "thank-yous" as Emmett left. As she closed the door behind him, anger began to replace her initial humiliation. There was no way she was going to allow Max Taylor to turn Almost A Wife into Almost A Scam! Charli grabbed her jacket and headed for the door.

CHAPTER ELEVEN

SHE nearly had a fender-bender with a small foreign car on her way into the garage of Taylor Enterprises. Charli pulled into the closest parking spot, ignoring the fact that it was marked Reserved.

If Max had engineered this marriage just to secure a place on Emmett's board, then he'd also known perfectly well from the outset that their marriage would have to be a permanent one. Emmett would not be charmed with an on-again, off-again marriage.

As Charli stomped into the elevator, she realized that she was still wearing blue jeans and a T-shirt on which she'd painted experimental butterflies with puff paints. Again, she'd sabotaged herself with ridiculously casual clothing when entering Max's world. But it was too late now. She was going to have it out with him no matter what.

"Hello, there, Mrs. Taylor," Dora greeted Charli when she barreled through the door to Max's office. "What a darling shirt. Where did you get it?"

"I made it." Charli's hand drifted absently across her middle. "I was working on a project to use at a child's birthday party."

"You are so clever," Dora went on. "I was telling Mr. Taylor just yesterday what a delightful woman he'd married..."

"Speaking of Max, is he in?"

"No. He said he had a luncheon meeting."

"Oh." Charli visibly deflated.

"But he usually makes such appointments at the Marine Club around the corner. I'm sure if it's an emergency, you can find him there."

"It's an emergency, all right," Charli muttered, but she smiled at Dora as she backed out the door.

The Marine Club was a popular restaurant with a nautical theme. There were portholes instead of windows, anchors and thick ropes littered about, and staff in crisp, navy-and-white uniforms inside the club. Most of the customers wore dark suits and sombre expressions.

"If this is what high finance looks like, I'm glad I don't have anything to do with it," Charli muttered to herself. The people Max knew and dealt with all looked pompous, stuffy and worried. All, of course, except for Walker. And when she'd left him, even he had looked plenty worried.

"May I help you?" the host intoned. She had epaulets and little stars on her shoulders. What did that make her? Captain? First Mate?

"I'm looking for someone. Max Taylor."

"Is he expecting you?"

"Not exactly."

"If you'd like to look around, go ahead. There are several small rooms off the main dining room. Perhaps he's in one of those."

Charli gave the woman a grateful smile and hurried into the large dining room. Max was not there; nor was he in the first of the tiny salons. Charli poked her head through the doorway of the second salon and pulled it back just as quickly. Then she peered more carefully around the thick burgundy drape that had been pulled to one side of the doorway.

She'd found him. And a whole lot more.

Max was lifting his glass—obviously a sparkling wine by the volume of bubbles in the flute—to a lovely blond woman dressed in a crisp, umber-colored business suit that somehow managed to showcase every one of the woman's voluptuous curves.

The woman laughed and raised her glass to his. The edges clinked together with a clear pinging sound. They they both drank, their gazes never breaking.

Charli didn't wait to hear or see more. Her tolerance level for the type of intimate tête-à-tête she'd just seen was nil. She hurried through the club and raced out the door, nearly wiping out a portly gentleman carrying an umbrella. With trembling hands, she started her car and steered it toward home.

Home. Could she still call it that? Could she call it anything else? It was the only place she had to go. She'd turned her own apartment over to her mother. The Almost A Wife offices weren't set up for overnight guests. She'd given up *everything* to move into Max's house. The enormity of the commitment she'd made to him finally began to sink into her consciousness. She'd sacrificed everything to play pretend house with Max and now she had nowhere to go.

"Real" marriage or not, she would not be toyed with or cheated upon or made to be a laughingstock. Yet Max had done all three.

She stormed through the house with tears streaming down her cheeks, her fingers itching to throw things. She picked up the wedding gift the Emmetts had given her, an intricately designed hand-blown piece of glass in the shape of a heart. She stuffed it in the trash. It wasn't a symbol of her marriage, but of the hollow feeling inside Charli.

She was so engrossed in her fury that she didn't hear Max's car on the driveway or his key in the lock. She jumped when his voice found her in the dim recesses of the living room.

"Charli? Are you here? Dora said you came by the office looking for me and that she sent you to the club to find me. Is something wrong?"

Was something wrong?

A rasp of pained laughter bubbled out of her. A better question might be, *Was anything right*?

"Everything is hunky-dory, just dandy, fine as can be, thank you." She spun around to face him, not caring if he saw the tears on her cheeks. "I want a divorce."

"What's happened? Why are you so upset?" As he moved toward her, she jumped back as if he brandished a hot poker.

"I don't like being lied to and I won't be used against my will. At least when you hired me to be Almost A Wife, you were honest, but now you've gone too far."

"I don't understand..." He sounded genuinely puzzled, a tribute to his acting capabilities, Charli thought.

"Then let me spell it out for you. I want out of my contract. *Finis*. End. No more. I can take care of everything except explaining to your friends what went wrong in our little love nest. You can do that. You're the expert at making up lies."

Charli raced past him to the staircase and was halfway up the stairs before the stunned Max managed to turn around and come after her. She ran into her bedroom, slammed the door and locked it. She was still leaning against it heavily when Max began to pound on the other side.

"Open this up right now! We need to talk."

"I've talked all I want to talk."

"Charli, I don't know what this is about, but..."

"You're a Rhodes scholar, figure it out."

"You can't break our deal now, Charli. I need you."

"Too bad. You lie and you can't keep promises, Max Taylor. And you're probably a *crook*, too! If you think it's expensive to buy a marriage, wait until you see how much it costs you to buy a divorce."

She'd said that just for effect. She knew that Max was perfectly scrupulous in all his business dealings. Still, the statement's effect on Max was startling. She heard a fist slam into the door.

Wide-eyed, Charli backed away. Why was he taking this so hard? *She* was the one who'd been lied to. She was the one who'd been turned into a fool. He'd had a champagne lunch with a beautiful woman when he was supposed to be newly and happily married!

She took a tentative step toward the door. It was very quiet on the other side. Had he hurt his hand? Gone for a key? Left the house? Charli didn't know. Strangely enough, angry and hurt as Max had made her, she still actually cared.

The sound of the doorbell made Charli rush to the window to see who was on the front porch. As she peered through the pane, she saw Walker Calhoun stepping inside.

"Problems?" Walker asked the roaring mad Max.

"It was a stupid idea. I should never have gone through with it," Max lamented, pacing.

"Does this ranting have anything to do with a certain lovely lady who only a few weeks ago had made your life perfect?"

"Women," Max snarled. "I should have known better than to think it would be any different."

"Any different than what?" Walker asked, then immediately followed with another question. "You're not comparing Charli to other women, are you?"

"She only married me for my money," Max growled. "It's been five days and already she's ready to leave and take me for every penny I'm worth."

"Charli?" Walker's mouth dropped open. "You're all wrong, Max. She's as close to perfect as you're going to find."

"Ha! That's what you think. You haven't lived with her."

"Don't I wish I had."

Again Max scowled.

"Look, you're all wrong about Charli, Max. I don't know what kind of disagreement the two of you had, but nothing's going to convince me Charli's a gold digger. She loves you."

"Yeah, right."

"It's true. She admitted it to me. Said she felt like a fool because she knew you didn't love her."

Max considered Walker's statement in silence.

"If it were me, I'd make sure I knew all the facts before I made any hasty decisions," Walker advised. "Don't be a damned fool."

As Walker rose to leave, a shimmer of light caught his eye. He bent to retrieve the glittering object from the trash. "Did someone misplace this?" he asked.

Max eyed the glass heart curiously. He sifted through the packaging material in the trash can to find Franklin Emmett's note. He read it aloud. "'To Max and Charli, whose marriage has made it possible for me to appoint the newest board member....'"

"Damn." Max grimaced. "Charli must have seen this. That's what this is all about."

Walker clicked his tongue. "So she finally figured out why you needed a wife."

Without a word, Max turned and raced up the stairs. Walker quietly let himself out.

"Charli? I want to talk to you." Max pounded on her bedroom door.

"Go away. Leave me alone." Her voice was ragged with tears.

"I've got something I must explain to you."

"Don't bother. I've already heard enough lies from you to last a lifetime."

"You don't understand..."

"I understand perfectly. That's why I won't come out and why I want a divorce. I understand that you married me just so you could worm your way onto FutureTec's board. I understand that you spend your business lunches sipping champagne with beautiful women who aren't your wife. I 'understand' plenty, Max. I don't think I can take any more 'understanding' right now."

He looked helplessly at the door. He could break it down, he supposed. That wouldn't be hard. The difficult part would be getting past the barriers Charli was erecting around her heart.

"I'll wait till you come out, Charli. Then we'll talk. I don't care how long it takes. When you're finished, I'll be waiting."

Charli huddled on the other side of the door, tears streaming down her cheeks.

She didn't know how long she'd been there, curled into a fetal position against the doorjamb. She must have fallen asleep. The sky outside was getting dusky. The sun would be setting soon. She had to get up. She had to move, to take some action.

She rose stiffly, wincing at the pains in her joints and the dull ache in her head. She licked her lips and could taste the salt of her tears on them. As she passed by the mirror, she glanced at her pain-ravaged face and grimaced. Look what Max Taylor had done to her!

Charli turned on the faucets, dropped her clothes into a messy puddle on the floor and stepped into the shower.

Downstairs, Max heard the water begin to run. He breathed a sigh of relief and turned up the oven.

The shower had done little to revive her spirits, but at least her muscles had lost some of their stiffness. Charli grabbed the first garments she saw in the closet and put them on. She raked her fingers through her damp hair and the dark curls sprang to life.

When she reached the bedroom door, she put her ear against it and listened intently. There was no sound whatsoever. No footsteps, no radio, no movement at all that she could hear.

"Maybe he's left," she said aloud. Even the sound of her own voice made her head ache. She had never cried so much or so long before. She felt drugged, dry and empty.

Cautiously she opened the door.

He was not in the hallway. The doors along the hall were open and the rooms were empty. Charli didn't want to take time to pack. Max could have her belongings sent to her mother's home later. Or he could keep them, for that matter. There was nothing there of enough value to risk ever having to see him again.

Tiptoeing, Charli made her way down the hall, always alert for signs that Max might hear her. Her purse was in the kitchen, lying on the counter. If she could get through there, she was home free. Her car was in the garage between Max's BMW and her shiny new Camero. *Home free*—but with no place to call home anymore.

As soon as she pushed on the swinging door which led to the kitchen, the aroma of roasting meat wafted into her face. She knew she'd made a tactical error.

Max stood in the middle of the kitchen wearing one of Charli's ridiculous aprons. His shirt sleeves were rolled to his elbows and he was holding a spatula in his hand. His dark hair was rumpled and there was a streak of chocolate across one cheek.

"Charli, I—"

"Don't say anything. Don't even look at me. Just let me get my purse and leave. I don't want your explanations. I'll have my lawyer contact your lawyer in the morning."

She moved into the kitchen and toward the far counter where she'd laid her purse. She was shocked to see that the kitchen table was set. A linen tablecloth covered the ceramic-tiled tabletop. Max's finest crystal and dishes were set into place settings for two. He'd moved a boom box into the eating nook and it was spilling out the soft sounds of Frank Sinatra. And the nook had changed completely. Dozens of red roses— in vases, pitchers and bowls filled the area, surrounding the table with lush, red velvet petals. There were roses on flower stands, on the extra chairs, even a couple dozen arranged with obvious care in the trash can.

"Wha—" Charli's features registered amazement. There had to be at least a thousand dollars' worth of roses in the breakfast nook.

Max moved from behind her to set a beautiful roast surrounded with new potatoes and baby carrots on the table. "I know you want to leave, but will you at least consent to having dinner with me first?"

"You did all this?" Charli asked in amazement.

"Do you like it?"

"You never needed Almost A Wife at all," Charli blurted. "Not if you can pull something like this together!" She looked at him with accusation in her eyes. "That was just one more lie."

"I didn't say I wasn't capable of fending for myself, Charli. I just said I was too *busy* to do it."

"You *never* needed me. I don't see why—"

"I've *always* needed you. I just didn't realize it, Charli, not until now, when I'm in danger of losing you."

Charli stood rock-still in the middle of the kitchen staring at him. "If you'd wanted to keep me, you should have told the truth."

"But I did."

"I didn't know that you married me to secure a position on FutureTec's board."

"I didn't."

"Then why..."

"I married you because I wanted to. I married you because I love you. I married you because I'd hoped that someday, with time, you could learn to love me, too. The spot with FutureTec was a bonus, not the motivating factor."

"I don't believe you."

Max dropped the utensil he was holding and moved forward. "Charli, FutureTec isn't what matters, *you* are. I've got all the wealth, power and influence I need. A spot with FutureTec would be a nice ego stroke, but nothing more. I can live without FutureTec. I can't live without you."

"But you..." She glanced up sharply, the import of his words just sinking into her consciousness. "You can't?"

"Not for a minute longer. I've lived a very lonely life, Charli. Part of that is my own fault. I watched my father suffer through a miserable divorce and decided then and there that it would never happen to me. I assumed that *all* marriages were suspect. I focused on my career instead. *You* were the one who taught me that there are more important things in life—and that love *can* be real."

Charli looked at him through narrowed eyes. "Like with beautiful blondes."

Max looked puzzled. "What do you mean?"

"I was in the Marine Club, Max. I saw you with that other woman." Charli hated sounding so shrewish, but that memory had been eating at her for hours.

"Do you mean Amy?"

"Is that her name?"

"It has been—at least since she married my younger brother."

Charli felt as though a load of bricks had fallen on her. She could barely catch her breath. "She's your sister-in-law?"

"She was in the city for an appointment. Amy often stops by the office to see if I'm free for lunch. I made time for her because tomorrow is her birthday."

"You were celebrating her birthday?" Charli remembered the bubble-filled flutes and the conclusions to which she had come.

"I don't understand why you just didn't come over and introduce yourself. It would have made things considerably easier. And you would have saved us both a lot of frustration."

"I thought..."

"You thought that just because I had lunch with another woman, it meant something romantic was happening."

Charli closed her eyes. "You're right. I did."

When she opened her eyes she was surprised to find Max grinning widely, as if she'd just given him a huge gift. "That means you cared," he said.

"Of course, I cared! I love—"

"Don't stop now, Charli, say it." Max's eyes glowed.

"I love *you*. I didn't want to. I fought against it, but it's true. I do love you. And that's what's made this thing with Emmett and with your sister-in-law so awful...."

"It's over, Charli. I'll call Amy and Gerr tonight and have them bring Jeremy in so you can meet them and see for yourself what Amy is to me. And then I'll call Franklin Emmett and tell him that I can't accept a position on his board."

"That's not necessary..."

"Maybe it is, Charli." He lovingly cupped the palms of his hands around her face and looked into her eyes with an expression of adoration so powerful and moving that Charli felt weak.

"I won't have *anything* standing in our way or making you believe that my love for you isn't genuine. I've waited too long for you, Charli. I never really expected to find you. I won't take any risk that might make me lose you now."

Charli moved into Max's arms and melted against him. "I *do* love you. I *do!*"

"Then you'll stay my wife? My *real* wife? For always and forever?"

Charli nodded and buried her face against his broad chest. "I'll never feel like 'almost' a wife again," she promised.

She felt him chuckle. "I'm glad you finally realize it, Charli. You will always be the *real* thing to me."

Take 4 bestselling love stories FREE

Plus get a FREE surprise gift!

Special Limited-time Offer

Mail to Harlequin Reader Service®

3010 Walden Avenue
P.O. Box 1867
Buffalo, N.Y. 14240-1867

YES! Please send me 4 free Harlequin Romance® novels and my free surprise gift. Then send me 6 brand-new novels every month, which I will receive months before they appear in bookstores. Bill me at the low price of $2.67 each plus 25¢ delivery and applicable sales tax if any*. That's the complete price and a savings of over 10% off the cover prices—quite a bargain! I understand that accepting the books and gift places me under no obligation ever to buy any books. I can always return a shipment and cancel at any time. Even if I never buy another book from Harlequin, the 4 free books and the surprise gift are mine to keep forever.

116 BPA A3UK

Name	(PLEASE PRINT)
Address	Apt. No.
City	State	Zip

This offer is limited to one order per household and not valid to present Harlequin Romance® subscribers. *Terms and prices are subject to change without notice. Sales tax applicable in N.Y.

UROM-696   ©1990 Harlequin Enterprises Limited

Harlequin Romance®
and Harlequin Presents®

bring you two great new miniseries with one thing in common—MEN!
They're sexy, successful and available!

You won't want to miss these exciting romances
by some of your favorite authors,
written from the male point of view.

Harlequin Romance® brings you

Starting in January 1998 with Rebecca Winters,
we'll be bringing you one **Bachelor Territory** book
every other month. Look for books by Val Daniels,
Emma Richmond, Lucy Gordon, Heather Allison
and Barbara McMahon.

Harlequin Presents® launches **MAN TALK**
in April 1998 with bestselling author Charlotte Lamb.
Watch for books by Alison Kelly, Sandra Field and
Emma Darcy in June, August and October 1998.

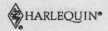 HARLEQUIN®   *There are two sides to every story...*
and now it's his turn!

As Seen on TV!

Free Gift Offer

With a Free Gift proof-of-purchase
from any Harlequin® book, you can receive
a beautiful cubic zirconia pendant.

This stunning marquise-shaped stone is a genuine cubic
zirconia——accented by an 18" gold tone necklace.
(Approximate retail value $19.95)

Send for yours today...
compliments of ✦ HARLEQUIN®

To receive your free gift, a cubic zirconia pendant, send us one original proof-of-purchase, photocopies not accepted, from the back of any Harlequin Romance®, Harlequin Presents®, Harlequin Temptation®, Harlequin Superromance®, Harlequin Intrigue®, Harlequin American Romance®, or Harlequin Historicals® title available at your favorite retail outlet, together with the Free Gift Certificate, plus a check or money order for $1.65 U.S./$2.15 CAN. (do not send cash) to cover postage and handling, payable to Harlequin Free Gift Offer. We will send you the specified gift. Allow 6 to 8 weeks for delivery. Offer good until December 31, 1997, or while quantities last. Offer valid in the U.S. and Canada only.

Free Gift Certificate

Name: _____

Address: _____

City: _____ State/Province: _____ Zip/Postal Code: _____

Mail this certificate, one proof-of-purchase and a check or money order for postage and handling to: HARLEQUIN FREE GIFT OFFER 1997. In the U.S.: 3010 Walden Avenue, P.O. Box 9071, Buffalo NY 14269-9057. In Canada: P.O. Box 604, Fort Erie, Ontario L2Z 5X3.

FREE GIFT OFFER   084-KEZ

ONE PROOF-OF-PURCHASE

To collect your fabulous FREE GIFT, a cubic zirconia pendant, you must include this original proof-of-purchase for each gift with the properly completed Free Gift Certificate.

084-KEZR